Brann and the *Iconoclast*

William Cowper Brann seated at his desk in the offices of
the *Iconoclast* in Waco

BRANN AND THE
ICONOCLAST

By Charles Carver

INTRODUCTION BY ROY BEDICHEK

AUSTIN · UNIVERSITY OF TEXAS PRESS

Second Printing

© *1957 by University of Texas Press*

Library of Congress Catalog Card No. 57–8822

Manufactured by the University of Texas Printing Division

FOR *Vicki* WITH LOVE

Contents

Contents

Illustrations

Introduction

 In our village school near Waco during the fall of 1895, *Brann's Iconoclast* was contraband. However, its format permitted it to be snugly fitted into the center of a school geography. Thus ensconced it was passed back and forth between me and an accomplice whose taste in literature was similarly "depraved."

The next fall (1896) I became a stenographer in a law office located on the same floor of the Provident Building as the business and editorial offices of the *Iconoclast*, in which I occasionally did stenographic service. This was genuine adventure. Almost any morning I could look across the intervening court and actually see the great man working at his desk. Although my regular employer, J. E. Boynton, whom I greatly admired, was generally on the opposite side, I became more and more committed to Brann's side (or sides) of his numerous controversies. I became a partisan, whole-souled and unconditioned.

Brann's flamboyant style was thrilling; his fearless and often excruciating lambasting of his opponents delighted me. His eloquence was charming although later and cooler judgment forces me to note that his perorations were often spotted with grandiloquence.

I witnessed the conclusion of the Scarborough whipping and, at this moment, can visualize Brann standing up, "head bloody but unbowed," waving his arms and shouting, "Truth will prevail," or some such slogan as he drove away from the scene of the encounter. I also saw the conclusion of the Harris-Gerald duel.

But in February of 1898 right during the heat of the Baylor-Brann imbroglio, and only two months before the pistol shots were fired which ended it all, my contact was suddenly broken off. The rest is silence, or hearsay, or occasional recounting of incidents which had gradually lost warmth and intimacy in the sixty intervening years—until just the other day when the manuscript of this volume came into my hands.

Mr. Carver's book is a penetrating and intensive study of William Cowper Brann in his maturer years: his ideals, his emotional reactions, his peculiar mentality—all formed by his education by hard knocks—and, as the title of the work implies, it focuses on his final publishing venture with its impact upon a Texas community in the closing decade of the last century.

Shortly after the first Waco issue of the *Iconoclast*

appeared, a "renegade priest," one Slattery, denounced the Catholic Church in scathing terms before a large audience. From the floor Brann sharply disputed Slattery's statements, and an angry colloquy followed. This is the "germ action of the play."

Brann's challenge was elaborated, buttressed, and venomized in the next issue of the *Iconoclast*, and included also was an attack upon "Baptist hypocrisy," invidiously compared with the holy work and wisdom of the institution Slattery had traduced. Waco was a Baptist stronghold, seat of the oldest and most revered college of that denomination in the state. In the ensuing war of words—charge and countercharge, allegations and denials, and bitter back talk—a raw religious factionalism of ancient lineage was localized and exacerbated in an overwhelmingly Protestant community. It was a bruising controversy: inflammation set in and infection spread. While there is much else of interest and significance in this book, the mortal feud between Brann and Baylor thus initiated runs like a scarlet thread through the whole of it.

"It is safe to say," reads an editorial in the *Iconoclast* of April, 1895, "that should an apostate Protestant publicly prefer the same sweeping charges against the clergy and the female members of their flocks that Slattery prefers against the priests and nuns, no power between the two oceans could prevent him [*sic*] being torn to pieces and his foul carcass fed to the buzzards." Thus in this somber drama, the protagonist unwittingly predicts his doom, not only identifying his own transgression but forecasting the penalty awaiting him in the womb of Fate. Not unaware, I am sure, of the overtones here of Aeschylean tragedy, the author connects in iron-linked sequences the prophecy with its fulfillment—step by step as if marching to a predestined goal.

Shortly before the final curtain, as so often occurs in a stage play, a short breathing spell, a sense of security, a deceptive and beguiling peace settles down upon this man's stormy life. The facts of biography spotlight and sustain a dismal thesis, like the close of a Thomas Hardy novel—a thesis formulated in four words by the great pessimist himself: "Life offers—to deny." In Carver's skillful hands it makes a powerful presentation.

Succeeding issues of the *Iconoclast* found other institutions to defend besides the Catholic Church, other men and measures besides Slattery and the A.P.A. to denounce and exercise a malicious wit upon, other theories to discuss, and other themes and incidents of sufficient salacity to sell. The feud with Baylor had simmered down and might now have simmered out but for the Antonia Teixeira incident. This gave Brann the whiplash he proceeded to apply with unmitigated fury. It is the kind of thing that happens in the best regulated homes and institutions, in school and out, but hardly ever with features lending themselves to such spectacular dramatization. Brann played it for all it was worth and more, not only to boost circulation but to feed fat the ancient grudge he bore the institution involved.

Rationally considered, this bastinadoing of Baylor was based on the commonest of logical errors: that of generalizing not only from too few particulars, but of preferring a wholesale indictment upon a single particular. From this one terribly sordid affair, Brann proceeded to damn, to damn utterly and to damn continually, the whole administration of an institution that had been rendering distinguished service to Texas education for half a century. Logically the pyramid of his indictment stood upon its apex, but the scandal, artfully sex-seasoned, swept the state like a hurricane. This was yellow journalism in the raw.

On the other hand, Baylor, lacking the services of a modern expert in public relations, was unable to divert or dilute the ferocity of the attack. The offense outmaneuvered the defense at every point. Brann assumed the role of a knight in shining armor valiantly defending the honor of a defenseless child deeply wronged by those who stood in a parental relation to her. He simply reduced the defense to the self-damning expedient of publicly denouncing Antonia, a child in years, as a worthless waif if not, indeed, a born pervert gifted diabolically with the art of corrupting grown men with whom she was associated. This is the burden of President Burleson's reply (published herein) to Brann's indictment, and it could not, from the stand-

Brann and the *Iconoclast*

Prologue

They wouldn't let him rest—
even in his grave.

The grass had scarcely begun to cover the fresh-
turned earth when a skulking figure, gun in hand,
stole through Oakwood Cemetery one night toward
the carved marble lamp that marked the plot. By the
light of a Texas moon the man read the word "Truth"
cut into the lamp's base, and he stood a moment staring
at the profile carved in stone on the pedestal beneath.

It was a lifelike profile, sensitive and arrogantly
stubborn. Some considered it the image of a muckrak-
ing atheist, others that of a second Shakespeare. During his lifetime he was called saint, Devil's apostle, infidel, and a man with a spark of divine guidance.
Whatever the appropriate description, it remains still
the face of a writer whose pen not only turned brother
against brother in faraway England but so split a

3

Texas town into fist-fighting, gun-toting factions that finally, on April 1, 1898, a bullet ripped into his back "right where the suspenders crossed" as he walked down a sunny street.

The figure with the gun stepped back from the monument, kicking a container of flowers to one side. He raised his pistol in the silent cemetery and took aim at the bas-relief temple. With a curse at the dead man he pulled the trigger, and the report echoed eerily among the marble angels and weathered stone.

It was the last and least painful shot ever fired at William Cowper Brann. But the macabre gesture was an appropriate footnote to the career of a journalist who had poured out such a hypnotic brew of raw humor, blazing prose, and corrosive satire that a hundred thousand readers from England to Hawaii mourned his murder.

And the drums and trumpets of the little brass band that led his funeral procession three miles to the grave simply marked a pause in the bitter controversy that still, more than fifty years later, colors the cheeks and raises the voices of his friends and enemies alike.

A man without formal education, a man tall in body and mind, William Cowper Brann has yet to achieve his full stature as perhaps the last of the long line of vigorous independent pamphleteers whose origins stemmed from Grub Street. With the formalization of the newspaper profession, minds such as his have been relegated to "columns" in great newspaper chains, their influence watered down and shouldered aside by wire-service accounts of the latest revolution in Guatemala or the lady who found her first husband was alive after all.

In Brann's day there was a premium on thought per se. There was a premium on minds with fluency. It was the twilight era of the great popular essayists who provided stimulating dinner-table conversation not only for the Vanderbilts but also for the Joneses and the Smiths.

In a setting of general public interest in morals, in religion, in literature, and in affairs more reminiscent of Plato than of Post (Emily), Brann's mind and extraordinary writing ability burst upon the last decade of the 1800's like a rocket. The fact that the point of origin was a tiny, tin-roofed Texas town only made the event more impressive.

In constant rebellion against the hypocrisy of late Victorianism, Brann was able to fit mid-Texas events into the perpetually absorbing contest between right and wrong, good and evil. Such was his ability with evocative phrases and paragraphs and so stimulating was his viewpoint that he was read and cherished to the extent that his monthly *Iconoclast* became a bulletin men marveled at in Australia, Hawaii, Canada, and wherever thoughtful souls of humor gathered.

Readers with a penchant for the ironic, all neat souls whose contentment lies in deriving morals from the rewards or punishments of open mental rebellion will find satisfaction of one sort or another in the fable that was Brann's life. He lived fully and wrote vigorously what he believed, and the penalty for refusal to compromise with the idols of his time was a bullet in the back.

Who can measure the extent of the influence of a pamphleteer? Who can estimate the effect of a succinct line or a phrase burdened with intuitive wisdom on the mind of a young man or judge the effect on his philosophy?

Surely the life of a man so gifted as to bemuse a considerable segment of his thinking contemporaries deserves to be explored, and with a decent attempt at a fair balance between fact and conjecture.

The "Romish Conspiracy"

  Garland's Opera House and the Turf Saloon were separated only by a narrow alley, and this convenient adjacency smoothed the road to culture for many a citizen of Waco, Texas, in 1895. An added bit of thoughtfulness was the electric bell near the bar, which gave ample warning of curtain time. Thus the unhappy concertgoer could absent himself with decent brevity during intermission and return, suitably heartened, to his lady in good time for the rest of the program.

On the night of Thursday, April 25, the crowd at the Turf was exceptionally large. As groups of men in twos and threes left for the auditorium, others strolled in from the restaurant for a cordial before the bell rang. Gaslight gleamed hospitably from the prisms, glowed against the worn backs of the captains' chairs, and gave a belated wariness to the eyes of the stag heads mounted on the walls. A blue cloud of cigar smoke hung under the high ceiling, and the saloon was warm with deep laughter and male voices.

There were no ladies present, for tonight's lecture had been advertised FOR MEN ONLY by the speaker —Joseph Slattery, former priest and traveling tubthumper for the American Protective Association.

One of the least attractive organizations to flourish —even briefly—in America, the A.P.A. was an anti-Catholic, anti-Semitic secret society organized in Clinton, Iowa, in the early 1890's. Its members spread fears of a "Romish conspiracy" as they lectured in Omaha, Kansas City, Detroit, Buffalo, and other Northern cities. Capitalizing on the economic and political unrest of the South, the movement spread through Georgia, Tennessee, and parts of Texas.

Claiming two and a half million secret adherents, the A.P.A. at its height sponsored more than seventy weeklies devoted to printing abuse of the Catholics. It also subsidized lecturers who were advertised as "ex-priests" and "ex-nuns" who had escaped the tyranny of the Mother Church only just in time to save America from total corruption.

On the previous night Slattery had jolted his mixed audience by reporting that he personally had seen a true copy of a papal bull that called for a Protestant massacre "on or about the Feast of St. Ignatius in the Year of Our Lord 1893." As examples of Romish infiltration he had shouted that 60 per cent of New York

City's police force received their secret orders from the "diabolic Papal brain." He had claimed that seventy-three school boards in as many cities were controlled by Catholic members. And he asked his audience to consider just why their own President Cleveland had spent an hour and twenty minutes the week before with a committee of prelates.

Many of the men in the Turf Saloon had heard Slattery the night before, and they were unanimous in praising his abilities as a speaker. But there was a spirited lack of unanimity about the truth of his charges, chiefly because of an article that had appeared in the April issue of the *Iconoclast*, a brand-new periodical that had been started in Waco in February by a newcomer to the town named William Cowper Brann. When he learned of Slattery's lecture series, Brann alerted his readers as follows:

Ex-Priest Slattery and his ex-nun wife are still at large in the land, pandering to anti-Catholic prejudice and collecting money of cranks. We have in this country a large contingent of ignorant fanatics who really believe that the Roman Catholic church is intent on overturning the American government and supplanting the President with the Pope, who are quite sure that the priesthood is a colossal aggregation of rogues and the convents but cloaks for all manner of immorality. The fact that the Pope has frequently expressed his admiration for the American government; that every convocation of Catholic prelates in this country has breathed the spirit of patriotism and tolerance; that the

9

Catholics were among the first to establish religious liberty in the western world; that they have aided in the upbuilding of this mighty nation, have participated in its councils, supported it with their treasure in the hour of trial and bedewed its every battlefield with their blood—counts for nothing with these narrow-minded bigots, these hate-inflamed fanatics.

"Convince a man against his will,
He'll hold the same opinion still."

It is to this class, the class responsible for that un-American organization known as the A.P.A.—Aggregation of Pusillanimous Asses—that ex-Priest Slattery panders. There are probably bad priests and unchaste nuns. With some hundreds of Protestant preachers in our penitentiaries—and as many of their female parishioners branded as bawds—it were indeed remarkable if all priests were paragons of purity; but Slattery's sweeping denunciation is simply slander for which he would be promptly punished by due process of law did Catholic prelates consider him worthy their serious consideration. Slattery is becoming a white elephant on the hands of the American authorities. The Catholic prelates decline to prosecute him, while the laity attempt to stop his blackguard bazoo with a bludgeon. In protecting him the authorities realize that they are shielding a foul-mouthed calumniator and brazen adventurer, and that if they decline to do so they will be arraigned by the aforesaid Aggregation of Pusillanimous Asses for "permitting the Church of Rome to throttle the American right of free speech." It is safe to say that should an apostate Protestant publicly prefer the same sweeping charges against the clergy and the female members of their flocks that Slat-

10

tery prefers against the priests and nuns, no power between the two oceans could prevent him being torn to pieces and his foul carcass fed to the buzzards. The simple fact that Slattery is alive to-day is a glorious tribute to the Christian charity of the Roman Catholic Church.

On Wednesday night Slattery did not fail to reply in kind. He attacked the editor as a pope-lover and a sensation-seeker, and he threatened to sue for libel. Brann's comment was reported in Thursday's *Morning News:*

In his lecture last night ex-Priest Slattery gave Brann's Iconoclast a terrible turning over for something he said about him in the last number, and being a firm believer in fair play, the News hunted the "Apostle" up to see what he had to say about it.

"Yes, I heard it," replied the "Apostle" to the reporter's interrogatory. "It wasn't much of a 'roast'. Slattery is not up in the art of peeling the cuticle off an opponent. The pathetic is his great lay. He can't skin worth shucks."

"He said that the Iconoclast credited the Catholic Church with being the first to establish religious liberty in America. How about that?"

"The Iconoclast never said it. I'll give Slattery $500 if he'll find that in the Iconoclast. He made a great bluff by declaring that if I dared assail his moral character he'd 'make me prove it in the courts.' Now, if you'll tell me how to hit a man harder than I did Slattery, I'll be obliged. If he don't consider what I said about him in the April Iconoclast a reflection on his so-called

11

moral character, he's paper-bullet proof. Yes, I'm going to take a shot at him in the next Iconoclast, and to give the little man a chance while he's in town, to square himself, I'll send a summary of the article to him at the Opera House tomorrow night. I want to hear him howl."

Then the "Apostle" took a three-finger night cup and retired to his virtuous slumbers.

Word had spread that day that the battle of podium versus press might be climaxed by Brann's appearance at the Opera House to listen firsthand to Slattery's "howling," and this possibility considerably heightened the interest and attendance Thursday night.

By eight o'clock the last cordial had been downed, the bell had sounded, and the Opera House (at thirty-five cents lower floor, twenty-five cents gallery) held a capacity audience of 350 people. The proscenium was decorated on the right and left by large American and Texas flags in brass standards. In the center was a small walnut rostrum bearing a pitcher of ice water and a glass. The stage proper was hidden by an elaborate golden curtain.

When Slattery appeared, his dignified manner and dark suit made more than a modest amount of applause seem out of place, and it died quickly. A recently ordained Baptist minister, with a well-advertised eight years of active priesthood before that, Slattery was an engaging, capable speaker. There was no nonsense to his manner, for his message was one warning of grave danger to the country. Quietly, solemnly, and with disarming reasonableness he explained his mission of the evening—to discover to this "men only" group certain secret and shocking practices which were far too dissolute for the ears of respectable wives and daughters.

This promise enabled him to acquire the total and absorbed attention of his audience in less than thirty seconds.

Slattery forthwith delivered the prepared brew of bigotry, misinformation, and implication that the A.P.A. headquarters were currently supplying their speakers. His voice, when he described the "real" purpose of nunneries, was a salacious whisper. It cracked like a bullwhip as he traced a stream of gold from ten thousand poor boxes to the bulging vaults of the Vatican. And Slattery's tone was like a bugle as he reminded his audience of the religious freedoms for which their grandfathers had sacrificed their lives and fortunes.

He chose to use the alleged attempt by the Catholics to control the school system as a springboard for his leap upon the *Iconoclast*'s editor. "Now if I should say that there was one among you—a stranger to Waco, I hasten to add—who does everything in his power to divert justice from these perverters of your children, would you not color with shame for the reputation of your city?" Slattery shook his finger at the crowd. "Who is this pope-lover who seeks to subvert you? Is he a man of fame or honor? Is he a senator, perhaps, of years and wisdom?"

There was an expectant silence. Slattery's voice quivered with scorn. "No, my brothers, no! He is simply a pipsqueak scrivener who has soiled your city with a calumnious rag called the 'Iconoclast', a fetid tangle of lies and half-truths, hiding his slander behind altars and anti-Christ slogans! Not without cause did Thomas Dewitt Talmadge brand him the Apostle of the Devil! Not without justice did a one-armed citizen run him out of San Antonio with his whipped tail between his legs!"

There were shouts of "Bravo!" Men stamped on the floor until the Opera House shook. "Where is he?" someone cried. Slattery pulled a large white handkerchief from his pocket. He stood mopping his forehead and surveyed his work with a look of pleased detachment.

There was a stir toward the back of the house. A man had risen from his seat and stood quietly facing the speaker.

The audience saw a tall, handsome man calmly waiting for the noise to subside. His eyes were brown and direct, his brow wide. The set of his jaw gave him an expression of mild arrogance, which was softened by an amused curve of his full lips. Though his gray suit needed pressing and the dark waistcoat was wrinkled, there was a devil-take-you pride in the man's eyes and an exuberance in his bearing that brought an immediate, eager silence to the hall.

"It's no surprise to me that my Iconoclast does not please you, sir." Brann's voice was rich and strong. "Because its mission, as the name implies, is to expose frauds and fakes." He looked directly at the man on the rostrum. "As the old saying goes, Mr. Slattery, 'it's the hit dog that yelps loudest.' " There was a guffaw of laughter and a flurry of clapping. "I have never written or uttered a word disrespectful to any religion, Pagan, Protestant, or Catholic. I do not war upon religious faith, but upon falsehood; not upon Christ, but upon those who disgrace his cause by mistaking bile for benevolence and gall for godliness."

Slattery's face reddened. He advanced a step and gripped the rostrum with his hands. "If I had known in advance that my lecture was to become a debate," he said, "I would have doubled the price of admission." Laughter from the crowd. "Would you gentlemen prefer to hear the truth about the Roman Catholic Church this evening or shall I lower myself to refute the attack of a—" he gave Brann a mock bow "—gentleman who found it so hot in San Antonio that he decided to come north to Waco, where the climate was a little cooler?"

The house manager had approached Brann and was talking earnestly to him, but when Slattery made the reference to San Antonio, Brann jerked away angrily. He pointed his finger at the former priest.

15

"You lie and you know it!" he shouted. "I refuse to listen to you!"

Whereupon he walked leisurely to the door, stopped, blew a kiss to the lecturer, and disappeared from the hall. The remainder of Slattery's talk, although studded with spicy anecdote, was somehow anticlimactic.

Carlyle and the Courthouse Run

CHAPTER 2

Perhaps by design, Brann's well-reported attacks on Slattery and the A.P.A. were very good for the circulation of the May *Iconoclast*, and in that issue he took a parting shot at Slattery— and at those who encouraged the A.P.A.

Ex-priest Slattery and his ex-nun wife swooped down upon Waco recently and scooped in several hundred scudi from prurient worldlings and half-baked Protestants whose chief religious stock in trade is unreasoning hatred of that church which, through the long intellectual night known as the "Dark Ages," preserved to the world the message of our Lord Jesus Christ. Brother Fight-the-Good-Fight was out in force, and many a Baptist dollar went into the coffers of these brazen adventurers.... The audiences were representative of that class of so-called Christians which believes that everyone outside its foolish sectarian fold will go to Hell in a hemlock coffin—a national convention of the Salvation Army could scarce make such a showing of No. 6 hats. . . .

Prose such as this was hardly the type to endear an editor to his community, and citizens of Waco who either had ignored the newcomer or had never heard of him found themselves suddenly and uncomfortably involved with an obscure man who was building himself a powerful pulpit of ink and paper.

Who was he? Where did he come from? In a town of only 25,000 it didn't take long to establish the tall man's background. Bit by bit, it would be revealed for the most part in the *Iconoclast*.

They discovered that the trail which led William Cowper Brann to what Milo Hastings called a "little country town lost in the immensity of the Texas prairie" was an odyssey that began in Coles County, Illinois, and wound for thirty-nine years of poverty and discouragement through the eastern half of America.

When Brann was two his mother died, and his father, Noble J. Brann, a Presbyterian minister of very modest means, placed him and his sister in the care of a farm family named Hawkins. William and Mary Hawkins had a son named Marion, and it is reasonable to assume that the two boys were companionable, although Marion was older than Brann. But in the one account Brann wrote of a youthful escapade, he was alone, and so it is safe to assume that Marion was the less headstrong of the two. Brann told his readers:

At the age of ten I was so infatuated with locomotives that to get possession of one I stole an entire freight train. It was standing on the main track in my native village, the crew had abandoned it to investigate a big watermelon which the station agent had opened, and I improved the opportunity to penetrate the mysteries of the engineer's cab. I had no intention of meddling with the iron monster, but when I got my hand on the lever the temptation to set the big drivers in motion was too strong to be resisted. The train started so easily that it did not attract the attention of the hilarious crew in the freight-house until it went roaring across Flat Branch bridge and on towards Mattoon at a good round gait. I decided that I might as well be hanged for an old sheep as a lamb, and pulled the throttle open a little wider, whistling and ringing the bell for all the crossings and pretty much everything else in sight. A mule got on the track in front of me, and I was so fearful he would escape that I gave the lever another lusty pull. The train fairly bounded forward and the telegraph poles seemed thick as fence posts. I got the mule—spread him all over the smokestack. By this time I had the lever down among the tallow pots—was making the highest speed the machine was capable of. The great iron monster swayed and groaned, the cars seemed bowing to both sides of the right-o'-way, and I was delirious with joy. Mattoon was in sight, and I determined to go through the town like a whirlwind, on to Cairo and take a look at the two big rivers. I was leaning out of the cab window trying to make out the figures on the mile-posts when I was suddenly pulled by the ear. Instead of joining the watermelon debauch the conductor had lain down in the caboose and gone to sleep. When the "dog house" began to dance on one wheel he awoke and realized that there was something wrong. He crawled over the boxes at the imminent risk of his life to expostulate with the engineer. While he was bringing the train to a standstill I debated whether I should run away or go back home and take the worst licking of my life. The conductor solved the problem for me; I went back. I have a very vivid recollection of the events immediately subsequent thereto, but as they could not possibly possess that absorbing interest for the general public that they did for me I will let them pass.

Another incident that Brann recorded much later shows the heroic attempts at corrective measures made by the Hawkinses in the case of their exuberant charge. It sheds an interesting light on his foster parents.

When I was a little Sunday school boy, a school teacher named Decker tried to frighten me out of all my faults. Assuming a hideous disguise, he entered my bedroom and informed me that he was Satan himself. As I had been told that the Devil would get me for swearing, I was not much surprised. I said: "You're a hell of a looking devil, but I believe you're lying; I'll just call you with this iron boot-jack." Satan didn't "get behind me," but he got.

At thirteen, perhaps on the heels of a similar incident, Brann left the Hawkinses and worked in a hotel as bellboy in a nearby town. It was the first of a variety of occupations. At seventeen he was a traveling drummer for a printing concern, and before he reached twenty-one he had worked as painter and grainer, printer's devil, fireman on a Texas freight, brakeman on the International and Great Northern, pitcher on a semiprofessional baseball team, and manager of an opera company of forty persons.

In 1876, when he was twenty-one, Brann settled—temporarily—in Rochelle, Illinois, and on March 3, 1877, he married Carrie Belle Martin, one of a family of twelve children. Her parents, from Iowa, were both "physicians." In all probability her mother was a midwife.

A slender, auburn-haired girl with blue eyes and a down-to-earth outlook, Carrie Martin must have known that "Harry," as she called Brann, would not be content for long in Rochelle. Yet they began a family. On December 19 Inez Martin Brann was born, but it was not until 1883 that her father went to work as a reporter for the *St. Louis Globe-Democrat*, edited by Joseph Burbridge McCullagh.

Not long after, perhaps as a result of seeing Texas during his younger railroading days, Brann joined the staff of the *Galveston Evening Tribune*, and it was in Galveston that his second child, Grace, was born in 1886. In May, 1889, he became an editorial writer with the *Galveston News* at $25 a week. Later he went to the *Houston Post*.

Why so many papers, and why such a relatively brief career with each? Evidence suggests that Brann was too independent to submit himself to an editorial line. Time after time he forgot his duty to speak the owner's mind and instead wrote the truth as he himself saw it—and was promptly fired in consequence.

During these long years of apprenticeship Brann somehow found time to give himself a liberal literary education. While covering the hotel beat for one paper he discovered Shakespeare. He mixed the courthouse run for another paper with a study of Carlyle's essays. He discovered the stately paragraphs of Macaulay; he thrilled to the exhortations of Tom Paine. He even made a brief incursion into writing drama. In February, 1889, he registered three plays at the Library of Congress: *Cleon*, *That American Woman*, and *Retribution*.

In 1890, while he was employed by the *Post* in Houston, a domestic tragedy occurred in Brann's home. Inez, whom they had nicknamed "Dottie," was then a young lady of thirteen. She was the delight of her father's heart. There were several boys "in love" with her, and their attentions worried the parents until Brann felt compelled to take steps. He tells the story in an essay—published after his death—which reads like a cry of remorse. The style is quaint now, compared to the bulk of his writing, but it was written in pain of spirit and for his own eyes only.

. . . And so the days went by, toilsome yet happy days until, when scarce passed to her 'teens, the youthful swains began to sigh for her and bashful cast their tribute of flowers—such as they knew she loved—into

22

the open door, then blushingly retreat, fearing cold comfort from her imperious eyes. And one there was of her own age, who seemed to haunt the street, until the mother noticed it and said:

"Daughter, what does he ever near the house?"

And the father fretted and spoke harshly of the boy, and sharply to his child saying: "You do encourage the little fool to haunt the place. Speak to him no more." And the daughter made reply:

"Father, I never spoke to him, nor he to me." And she arose, and taking her music roll went forth and the boy followed her.

"Our daughter deceives us!" cried the father fierce with rage; and he followed the twain.

"You have deceived me, daughter!"

His voice was sharp, and, quailing before his wrath as though it were a blow, she gasped, "Oh, father!" and returned with him in silence to their home.

And the little mother fretted and lectured her; but she sat silent, brooding upon the great wrong, and the queenly eyes were full of tears that seemed frozen by her pride and could not fall.

They never fell. The gust of anger from the doting father's lips, the breath of doubt of her dear word, and her little heart seemed broken quite; the world seemed desolate. The father's good-night kiss; the mother's tender solicitude were in vain,—the wound was too deep to heal. And while they slept and dreamed sweet dreams of her fair future she poured her heart out to the good God, who never doubted her, and leaving a little note that was a wailing cry of hopeless pain, passed by her own fair hand to the great Beyond.

And the father kissed the dead lips of his first born

and knew that he had killed her. And ever in his heart there is a cry, "I killed her!" And night and day that cold, sweet face doth haunt him; and day and night he hears that piteous cry, wrung from his child when he broke her heart, "Oh, father!" and ever the little mother's lamentation goes up to heaven, "Our house is left unto us desolate!"

On the afternoon of July 25 Dottie had taken an overdose of morphine tablets that she found in the medicine cabinet. She was found in a hammock behind the house, and nearby, in her careful handwriting, was a note.

Dear Mamma:
Tomorrow this time I will be dead.
I took all of that morphine.
I don't want to live. I could never be as good as you want me to.
I was born for a rowdy and you would be ashamed of me.
I hope God will take me to Heaven.
Good bye till I see you and papa and Gracie in Heaven.
Give my love to Annie, Harrie, Tot, and Rob.
Give all my things to Gracie.
Good by for ever.

A few months after the death of Inez, a difference between Brann and the proprietor of the *Post*, R. M. Johnston, terminated Brann's association with that paper, and he moved his family to Austin. Here in the state capital Brann's long-standing dream of becoming the editor of a one-man crusading journal became a reality. Scraping together his small savings, he launched Volume One, Number 1, of the *Austin Iconoclast.*

Born from his interest in the fiscal policies of the country, the journal was designed primarily to promote an "inter-convertible bond-currency plan"—a palliative more sensible than most for the fearful economic convulsions from which the country was suffering. Much of Brann's editorial writing was on the pros and cons of bimetallism, the state of the national debt, the tariff regulations, and the general upheaval coincident with the industrial revolution. It was natural for all public-spirited men to take sides, since the issues, they were convinced, would decide the economic life or death of America.

To men who had stood in the bread lines after the panic of 1884, who had seen rioting workers shot down in Virginia and the coal fields of Pennsylvania, and who had watched the buying power of the dollar slip to a sickening low, fiscal questions were anything but academic. Political platforms stood or fell on their economic planks, and the air resounded with theories and policies designed to ameliorate (or aggravate) the enmity between rich and poor.

Brann's proposal, unlike many others, was sound enough to receive serious congressional consideration.

He developed his plan—his "infant"—while in Houston.

In the year of our Lord, 1891, I became pregnant with an idea. Being at the time chief editorial writer on the Houston *Post* I felt dreadfully mortified, as nothing of the kind had ever before occurred in that eminently moral establishment. Feeling that I was forever disqualified for the place by this untoward incident, I resigned and took sanctuary in the village of Austin. As swaddling clothes for the expected infant, I established the Iconoclast. . . . When the youngster made his appearance in this troublesome vale of financial buncombe and economic idiocy, it was given the ponderous title of "Inter-convertible Bond-currency Plan." It's a wonder the name didn't kill it; but, turned out to grass, it thrived and grew in grace. The infant was generally supposed to be an unholy cross between incipient insanity and a well developed case of confluent Populism; but when the bankers of Germany, assembled at Berlin, approved the little waif, the suspicion passed. Hon. Tom Johnson became the Congressional champion of some features of the plan, which now finds earnest advocates among all political parties. . . .

A governmental money that will automatically and infallibly adapt itself to the varying needs of commerce, preserve the equilibrium between the money-work to be done and the money available to do it, and thereby obviate all danger of either appreciation or depreciation of the purchasing power of the dollar, is universally conceded to be the great desideratum. To attain this I propose:

(1) That the government keep constantly on sale at all postoffices of the presidential class low interest-bearing bonds in denominations of $100 to $1,000, re-

deemable at the option of the holder in full legal tender currency.

(2) That this new currency be added to the general revenue fund, and paid out the same as other money, until currency bonds to the amount of $250,-000,000 be taken—the proceeds constituting a redemption fund—when such additions to the general revenue fund shall cease and not be resumed until, through bond redemption, the fund set aside for that purpose falls below the foregoing figure.

That's all there is to the Inter-convertible Bond-currency Plan. When there is too little money, the government will supply more; when too much, the government will absorb the surplus, and the equilibrium at all times be maintained. There could be no "money famines" and consequent enhancement of the purchasing power of the dollar; there could be no depreciation, caused by the pressure of a redundant currency for employment. The redemption fund would be an infallible indication of the monetary needs of the country. The volume of currency would be controlled by the natural laws of commerce—Congress could neither add to nor take from it a single farthing. The administration would be powerless to mint a single coin or print a dollar bill until notified by the nation, through the medium of the redemption fund, that it needed more money. Silver might become plentiful as in the days of Solomon and cheap as scrap-iron; gold might advance in value another 100 per cent., and only the fine arts be affected—the American currency would maintain the even tenor of its way, the dollar be "the same yesterday, today and forever."

Brann was assisted in his first publishing venture

by a man named Edwards, who probably supplied a good share of the working capital. Discouraged by the poor reception of the paper, Edwards withdrew his support in November, ending Volume One.

Unwilling to give up, Brann began Volume Two in March of the following year, 1892, and changed the name to the *Texas Iconoclast*. But the public did not flock to buy, and after a few faltering issues Brann turned the management over to a T. M. Bowers and returned to the *St. Louis Globe-Democrat* as a reporter. He had a wife and two children to support.

In November the future turned brighter. He was offered—and promptly accepted—the editorship of the *San Antonio Express*, whose editor, Harry Canfield, was leaving to edit a Chicago daily.

Early in 1894 Bowers left the *Texas Iconoclast*, and in March Brann, who was too occupied on the *Express* (and probably too poor to rescue his paper yet again), put the plant up for sale. It was bought for $250 by a young teller at the First National Bank of Austin. His name was William Sidney Porter.

Brann's relationship with the *Express* suffered a typical denouement. W. H. Brooker, a San Antonio lawyer, had slandered two of Brann's fellow employees on the *Express*, and Brann gave him a "roast" in the paper's columns. The owner of the paper, a man named Grice, felt it politic to publish an apology in a succeeding issue. This he did, and signed Brann's name to it.

Unable to persuade Grice to print any more on the

controversy, Brann visited the offices of the *San Antonio Daily Light*, hoping their columns might be opened to his side of the affair. Here he ran into Brooker himself, who was a husky one-armed man weighing 225 pounds, and there was a scuffle during which Brooker threatened to "blow his brains out."

Brann bought a gun and wore it ostentatiously until Brooker, after due thought, withdrew his threat. But Brann's rapport with Mr. Grice was no longer firm, and on July 28 he left the *Express*.

This was the low point—the lowest point, in fact. Brann had no way of knowing that the next disheartening jobless months were merely the humid calm before such a hot storm of bursting literary vigor, such a raging brew of blood and ink that a hundred thousand readers would gasp in astonishment. At the age of thirty-nine he could look in the mirror and see only a man who had lost job after job through an unwillingness to be silent when honesty ached for a spokesman. He saw a man already in the second half of life, who had led his family on an aimless hegira from one drab boardinghouse to another, from one strange city to the next, without ever coming to a roof of their own. He saw the bitter reward for all his quixotism in the made-over dresses Carrie wore so patiently; he heard it in the voices of employers who tactfully turned him away.

That summer Brann earned a sporadic living by lecturing. He spoke to ladies' reading clubs on literature, to veterans' organizations on patriotism, to any group who would pay him an honorarium for his services.

At last, the month before Christmas, 1894, Will Brann was invited to become an editorial writer on the *Daily News* in Waco, a town of 25,000 people on the banks of the Brazos River.

"The Athens of Texas"

  "The Athens of Texas" and
"Six-Shooter Depot" were both nicknames for Waco,
Texas, in 1894, and each sobriquet accurately reflected
a side of the town's personality.

"Athens" was appropriate because Waco was the
educational center of Texas. There was Waco Female
College, established by the Methodists, with 300 pu-
pils. There was the Catholic Academy of the Sacred
Heart, with 200. There was the Negro university
known as Paul Quinn, which had been established in
1872 by the African Methodist Episcopal Church, and
there was the famous Baptist institution known as Baylor University, which had an enrollment of 500 young
men and women. In addition to these four there were
many smaller private schools and business colleges.

"Six-Shooter Depot" was a title bought with the
blood of hot-tempered citizens who adjusted their dif-

31

ferences according to a relaxed interpretation of the dueling code of the Old South. In the days of the cattle drives following the Civil War, Waco lay close to the Chisholm Trail, and the town supplied the drivers with recreation, which often involved high-spirited killing of one another. This buoyant mood lasted through the century—as long as guns were a usual item of wearing apparel.

Originally an Indian village, then a fort, then a trading post, Waco had been laid out on a shallow crossing of the Brazos River a hundred miles south of Dallas. One of the early settlers operated a ferry service across the river, and later, in 1870, a single-span suspension bridge—at that time the longest in the world—was completed and put into service as a toll bridge.

Its hub location helped Waco grow, and the gentle climate of the valley made the land rich in cotton. In 1893, there were 120,000 bales marketed in Waco for an average price of 7¼ cents a pound. Woolen mills south of the town employed almost 500 people, and large numbers also worked at the cottonseed-oil mills, planing mills, and flouring mills. Because prevailing wages were infinitesimal, a large and unsavory "mill area" developed, where living conditions were primitive and harsh with poverty. This district, called Edgefield, was later to be responsible for the nurturing of Clyde Barrow.

The gentler folk lived on Provident Heights, an

area developed by a builder named Samuel Colcord, of New York. Here there were stately mansions, laced with carving and gingerbreaded with cupolas and gables in the best Victorian style. Here lived the agricultural and merchant princes in whose hands the past and the future of the city rested. In the main, theirs was an aristocracy based on two generations of wrested success rather than on ten generations of well-documented breeding.

Unaffected, impulsive, hard-living, shrewd—they were the bridge-building, bronco-busting, cheroot-smoking link between the Indian trader and the spatted financier. Their ladies led them, reluctant, to musicales and uplifting lectures. Their ladies kept them attentive to the arts and the amenities acquired in the seminaries of larger cities or from the current periodicals.

On the 10th of March, 1889, the discovery of hot artesian water under the city made Waco a spa, and no small part of the 25,000 population was composed of transients who came from other parts of the state to drink and bathe in the healing waters. A huge natatorio-sanatorium was built near the center of town. It featured "Turko-Russian departments, cold plunges, office, parlors, individual baths, tubs, pools, vapors, needles, sweat rooms, and cafe." In 1894 the restrictions on advertising were less rigorous than they are today, and the diseases advertised as curable at the Waco springs included "inflammatory and chronic

33

rheumatism, stiffened joints, sciatica, lumbago, muscular rheumatism, gout, eczema, salt rheum, p-s-o-r-i-a-s-i-s, erysipelas, scrofula, blood poisoning, syphilis in all forms, locomotor ataxia, epilepsy, paralysis following cerebral spinal meningitis, neuralgia, insomnia, hysteria, alcoholism, St. Vitus dance, . . . general debility, nervous prostration."

Partly to accommodate the visitors who came to be cured and partly to accommodate the horde of traveling salesmen who were an important part of the American scene of that era, Waco had a better than average share of large hotels and homes that had been converted into "family hotels." Rooms were $2.00 to $3.00 a day, and, although there were no adjoining baths, the most luxurious of the rooms had hot and cold running water piped in.

Waco was laid out in squares on the two banks of the Brazos River. East Waco was mainly residential; the town proper was on the west side. The streets running northwest were all numbered, beginning with First Street, which paralleled the river. The intersecting streets had names: Jefferson, Columbus, Washington, Austin, Franklin, Mary, and so on south.

Austin Street was the main thoroughfare. Wide and graveled, it ran at right angles to the river, near which it broadened into a great square dominated by a city hall of brick and stone. The city hall was an imposing, gabled building with a clock tower at its west end. Capping the tower was a cupola with the customary wrought-iron fence work fringing a tiny platform at the top. The square was the heart of Waco. Here, particularly on weekends, the farmers left their teams and wagons while they went to shop in the stores that formed the town.

The square was ringed with flat-roofed one- and two-story buildings where hardware, cloth, guns, boots, and buggy whips were sold by the townspeople to the farmers. There were restaurants and saloons and fish markets on the square. There were tanners and pecan-buyers and cottonseed-cake merchants. There were milliners and blacksmiths and real estate agents and bankers and sign-painters and cobblers.

Old men who claimed to have seen the murder of Chief Bowl during the Cherokee War of 1839 exchanged tall tales with comparatively young bloods from Houston who claimed to have been with Dick Dowling when he fought off the federal troops at Sabine Pass in 1863. Mexicans, Indians, Negroes, and whites sought shelter from the sun under the unbroken wooden canopies that shelved out over the sidewalk. On Saturday nights there was dancing and gambling and an occasional knifing or shooting, but for the most part the square was the site of easy good will and companionship.

Fourth and Austin exuded a more urban atmosphere. The buildings were no larger, but they were better built, and several were of stone. On the northeast corner was the Old Corner Drugstore, with its recessed entrance and the post in front covered with notices and posters. It was a favorite gathering place for the town doctors, and there was a slate inside where patients without telephones could leave messages for their physicians. Diagonally across from the Old Corner Drugstore was the squat stone Citizens National Bank, and a block beyond it the new Post Office, at Fourth and Franklin.

The people in this part of town were a strange mixture of city and country. Many of them wore boots and broad-brimmed cowboy hats, which were, however, seldom dusty or scuffed. They wore string ties or bow ties, and their clothes were pressed and of less rugged weave than the clothes worn a block to the east. The people walked more purposefully, with the solemnity of business folk who had carriages of their own and perhaps a typewriter to whom they could dictate their correspondence. Some of them were members of the Commercial Club, which was concerned with civic progress. In 1894 Waco was the sixth-largest city in Texas, and the Commercial Club was determined to see it fifth, at the very least, by the turn of the century.

Across the river from the square, on the east bank, were the pillared plantation homes, enduringly constructed of hand-molded brick. Clustered near each home were the smaller brick smokehouses, kitchens, springhouses, and servants' quarters.

In 1894 Waco had a particular distinction, which

it shared with Omaha, Nebraska, and which set the two apart from other cities in the United States. These two towns had city ordinances setting aside certain blocks where prostitutes would not be disturbed by the law. In Waco the area was a relatively small section of three or four blocks on North Second Street, and there was nothing to mark it from the rest of the town unless it was a kind of depressing and wan shabbiness. Although the "reservation," as it was called, was free from the city police, county officials levied periodic tribute from raids. The area was a distinct financial asset to the city physician, who received $2.00 twice a month for a cursory examination of each girl.

To offset the stigma of the reservation, Waco was widely known for having almost as many churches as saloons. While there was a generous share of Episcopalians, Methodists, and Catholics, the town was predominantly Baptist, in politics as well as in denomination. This proportion held up in the field of religious publications. Of the four monthly religious pamphlets issued in Waco, three were Baptist, while the fourth, *The Independent Pulpit*, was an inquiring journal with an interestingly liberal approach, edited by one J. D. Shaw, whose unique story deserves recording.

In the early 1800's Shaw, a tall, well-set-up man with an impressive beard and hair worn fashionably long, was pastor of the Fifth Street Methodist Church, one of Waco's most imposing houses of worship. Shaw

37

had been a captain in the Confederate Army. He was a man's man, he delivered excellent sermons, and his devotion to his large parish was fully reciprocated.

In 1883 a phrenologist named O. S. Fowler toured the Southwest and had occasion to make an appearance in Waco. A good phrenologist in those days was certain to attract an outstandingly large audience, and Professor Fowler was no exception. The professor did more than simply explain his craft with the aid of charts— he was brave enough and showman enough to single out members of the audience and deduce their characters from the conformations of their skulls. In a loud voice he would report not only what the tips of his sensitive fingers discovered of the past but also what they foretold of the future.

Everyone present at the Professor's Waco appearance was highly amused when he selected their beloved Dr. Shaw from the audience and announced that he would publicly open the gates of tomorrow for him. Their amusement changed to horror, however, when Professor Fowler gravely explored the Reverend Shaw's skull for a few moments and then announced in a clear tone, "I find this man to be a skeptic in matters of religion!"

Coincidence or not, some months later Shaw did turn "modernistic," in that he publicly expressed doubt about the Biblical miracles. He became a freethinker, resigned from his pastorate, and organized the Religious and Benevolent Association of Waco. The association operated Liberal Hall, a frame structure at Seventh and Washington, where Sunday discussion sessions were held in lieu of the more conventional church services.

Two years later Professor Fowler returned in triumph for a second engagement in Waco, but there is no record that he was able to cap his first extraordinary prediction. Dr. Shaw died later in California, but his body was returned to Waco for burial.

Thus the Waco that Brann found in 1894 may have been a small town, and it may have been a prairie town, but it was also a religious and educational center bursting with intellectual as well as physical energy, as witness the schools and the more than fifteen periodicals that were regularly being issued in 1894.

In such an atmosphere it seems more logical than surprising that a man with a reporter's background and an argumentative, restless intellect should again be encouraged to publish a forum of his own, undismayed either by his earlier failure in Austin or by the intense competition that faced him in Waco. And so, in February, 1895, without backing of any kind, the first issue of the revived *Iconoclast* was presented to a mildly startled public.

Attack—and Sell

Volume V, Number 1, dated February, 1895, was a two-column pamphlet of sixteen pages and measured 8 by 11½ inches. It sold for one dollar a year, or ten cents a copy. It was hand-set, of course, and was published by the Knight Printing Company, at 209 South Fourth Street.

Brann was penniless when he came to Waco in November, 1894, and his salary on the *Daily News* was not princely. Therefore, according to reports of his associates at the time, his arrangement with the printing company was financially delicate. The press run for the first issue was two thousand copies, and eyewitnesses say that Brann rushed out with the first fifty copies under his arm, sold them to newsstand proprietors on the streets and in the hotels, then hurried back with the money and picked up another armload. Working in his favor was his reputation for trenchant writing in the *Waco Daily News*, and in addition he had a reasonably substantial reputation as a lecturer in the region.

The editor laid down the platform of the *Iconoclast* in its first Waco issue. The statement was deceptively reasonable and moderate:

The *Iconoclast* makes war upon no religion of whatsoever name or origin that has fostered virtue or added aught to the happiness of the human race. It is simply an independent American journal, exercising its constitutional prerogative to say what seemeth unto it best, without asking any man's permission.

Brann lost no time in exercising his prerogative vigorously. His readers found that he was either *for* something 100 per cent or *against* it 100 per cent. He never straddled an issue. His very opening article, published in an old-line Baptist stronghold, was a plea for religious tolerance. In a city that reverberated every Sunday to the message from fifty pulpits that salvation was to be found in One Book only, Brann wrote:

The Sacred Books of all the centuries are essentially the same—the half articulate voice of the world crying for light, the frantic efforts of man to learn whence he came and whither he goes, to lift the veil that shrouds the two eternities—to see and know! I gather them together—the old testament and the new, the Koran and the sacred Vedas, the northern Sagas and the southern mythologies; I search them through, not to scoff, but to gather with reverent soul, every gleam of light that since the birth of Time has been vouchsafed to man. I read the Revelations and ponder the Prophecies; I listen once again to the voice in the burning bush and the mystic whisperings of the Dodona Oak; I descend into the Delphic cave, or stand with uncovered head to hear the voice of Mennon answer to the rosy fingers of the morn. I sit with Siddartha beneath the Bodhi tree and follow the prophet of Islam in all his pilgrimages; I stand with Moses on Sinai's flaming crest and listen to the prayer of Christ in the Garden of Gethsemane, then I go forth beneath the eternal stars—each silently pouring its stream of sidereal fire into the great realm of Darkness—and they seem like the eyes of pitying angels, watching man work out, little by little, through the long ages, the mystery of his life.

This was prose to raise the hackles of every Baptist minister and earnest member of the Baptist faith, and there were tens of thousands in the area. The very popular DeWitt Talmadge, whose published sentiments were syndicated in over 3,500 newspapers, had christened Brann "the Apostle of the Devil" for expressing similar sentiments in the past.

And the Apostle did not ignore Talmadge in his first issue.

The Tyler *Telegram* humbly apologizes for having called that wide-lipped blatherskite, T. DeWitt Talmadge, "a religious faker." Next thing we know our Tyler contemporary will apologize for having inadvertently hazarded the statement that water is wet. When a daily newspaper tells the truth, even by accident, it should stick to it instead of crawling on its belly in the dust to humbly ask pardon of the Devil. The *Iconoclast* will pay any man $10 who will demonstrate that T. DeWitt Talmadge ever originated an idea, good, bad or indifferent. He is simply a monstrous bag of fetid wind. The man who can find intellectual food in Talmadge's sermons could acquire a case of delirium tremens by drinking the froth out of a pop bottle.

Also in the first issue of the *Iconoclast* in Waco Brann wrote an article entitled "The Buck Negro," which reflected the hysteria that had existed in the South since the end of the Civil War. These selections from "The Buck Negro" did not lose readers for subsequent issues:

I once severely shocked the pseudo-philanthropists by suggesting that if the South is ever to rid herself of the Negro rape-fiend she must take a day off and kill every member of the accursed race that declines to leave the country.... We have tried the restraining influence of religion and the elevating forces of education upon the Negro without avail . . . but the despoilment of white women by these brutal imps of darkness and the devil is still of daily occurrence. The baleful shadow of the black man hangs over every Southern home like the sword of Damocles, like the blight of death—an avatar of infamy, a decree of damnation. . . . We must consider ourselves first, others afterwards. The rights of the white man are paramount, and if we do not maintain them at any cost we deserve only dishonor. . . . There are too many long-haired men and short-haired women picking up a more or less honest

43

livelihood by experimenting with Sambo at our expense, his wonderful "progress," his divine "rights" and his devilish "wrongs," to permit serious consideration of what is really best for him. . . . The greatest injury ever done the people of the South was self-inflicted—the introduction of Negro slavery. The next greatest was the act of the Federal Government in making the black man coordinate sovereign of the state. . . . The presence of the Negro in the South has kept this section a century in arrears of what it would otherwise be. It has prevented white immigrations; it has kept out capital; it has bred a contempt among the Southern whites for labor; it has fomented strife between sections and is still fostering provincial prejudice, fanning the fires of sectional hate. . . . The Negro is, for a verity, the *Bete Noire* of the South, a millstone about her neck, tending ever to drag her down into the depths of social and political degradation. . . . The Negro will remain right where he is, wear the cast off clothes of the white man, steal his fowls, black his boots, rape his daughters, while the syphilitic "yaller" gal corrupts his sons. Yes, the Negro will stay, stay until he is faded out by fornication—until he is absorbed by the stronger race, as it has absorbed many a foul thing heretofore.

That Brann was well aware of the circulation value of inflammatory writing—such as the above—can be ascertained from a paragraph that appeared under "Fact and Fancy" in his first *Iconoclast*. It was a statement backed by the authority of more than a dozen years in the newspaper business.

Print the grandest sermon that ever fell from Massillon's lips of gold, and not twenty per cent, even of the professedly pious, will read it; print a detailed account of an international prize fight and ninety-nine per cent of the very elect make a dive for the paper before breakfast—will swoop down upon it like a hungry henhawk reaching for an unripe gosling and fairly devour it, then roll their eyes to heaven like a calf with the colic and wonder what this wicked old world is coming to.

Brann had arrived at a journalistic truth—that dissent, a sharp attack upon the status quo, was the surest way to acquire a following and to sell newspapers. In Waco the established targets were the Baptists, and from the first he joyfully ridiculed those of that faith whom he felt to be particularly narrow in their religious outlook. Brann objected to the zealous proselytizing that was an important part of the Baptist church. His argument was that charity—religious benevolence —should begin at home.

For a specimen of audacity that must amaze Deity commend me to a crowd of pharisaical plutocrats, piously offering in a hundred thousand dollar church prayers to Him who had not where to lay His head; who pay a preacher $15,000 per annum to point the way to Paradise, while children must steal or starve, while women must choose between death and dishonor, and men reared at Christian mothers' knees are driven by grim despair to curse the God who made them, and plunge into a career of crime. Everywhere the widow is battling with want, while these pharisees send Bibles and blankets, salvation and missionary soup to a job-lot of lazy niggers, whose souls ain't worth a sou-markee in blocks of five—who wouldn't walk into Heaven if the gates were wide open, but once inside would steal the eternal throne if it wasn't spiked down. Let the heathen rage; we've got our hands full at home. I'd rather see the whole black-and-tan aggregation short on Bibles than one white child crying for bread. . . . That religion which sits up nights to agonize because a few naked niggers in equatorial Africa never heard Eve's snake story, how Job scratched himself with a broken pie-plate, or the hog happened to be so full o' the spirit of Hades; that robs childhood of its pennies to send prayer-books to people whose redemption should begin with a bath, while in our country every town from Cape Cod to Kalamazoo, every city between the Arctic Ocean and the Austral sea is filled with "heathen" who know naught of the grace of God or the mystery of a square meal; who prowl in the very shadow of our temples of justice, build their lairs in proximity to our public schools and within sound of the collect of our churches, is an arrant humbug—a crime against man, an offense to God, a curse to the world.

Brann returned to the attack in the very next issue of the *Iconoclast*, and his target was the monthly *Baptist Standard*, edited by a Dr. J. B. Cranfill. In an article entitled "A Brotherly Rebuke" and headed "to the faithful in Texas, greeting," Brann assumed a tone of grief and bewilderment.

There are many things of which I would speak to

you; but what lies heaviest on my heart is the fact that most, if not all the religious contemporaries of the *Iconoclast* are in the habit of ladling out saving grace with one hand while raking in the shekels with the other for flaming advertisements of syphilitic nostrums, "lost manhood" restorers and kindred quack remedies for diseases with which the faithful are supposed to be unfamiliar. It grieves me to note that the purveyors of "panaceas" for private diseases regard the religious press as the best possible medium of reaching prospective patrons. Why this is so, I know not; but so it is, as every publisher in all the land doth right well know. . . . Still, it doth grieve the Apostle sore to see his brother ministers acting as bell-ringers for quack doctors and assiduously shoving degrading advertisements into the faces of decent people, regardless of age or sex. It shocks his sense of the proprieties to see a great religious journal (see "Editorials by Our Subscribers"—none of whom, we hope, have misplaced their "manhood") like the Texas *Baptist Standard* flaunting in the middle of a page of jejune prattle anent the Holy Spirit, a big display ad. for the "French Nerve Pill"—guaranteed to re-stallionize old roues— and following up a long dissertation on "The Weakness of the Baptist Denomination" with an illustrated notice to the effect that "loss of manly power resulting from bad habits" is cured by certain eastern Cagliostros, who will send, "securely sealed in plain envelope on receipt of 10 cents," a medical treatise "written in plain language." Perhaps the Apostle is entirely too sensitive where the reputation of his brethren in Christ is concerned; but it does grate upon his nerves to see a really good sermon in the Texas *Baptist* and *Her-*

47

ald flanked by an advertisement of "Pennyroyal Pills" —especially designed to produce abortions! . . . Of course it is difficult in times like these, when the people are far more interested in the price of pork than in forms of baptism for a professional peddler of piety to decline a fat fee proffered by the "Powers of Hell"; still we should ever bear in mind that while in this world we are not of it and be willing to subsist on corn bread and buttermilk here on earth that we may have pie and pound cake hereafter. We should not attempt to straddle the game, to serve two masters in the same column after this manner:

> Remember the Sabbath day to keep it holy.
> *Ladies, Pennyroyal Pills are Safe and Sure.*
> Believe and be baptized and ye shall be saved;
> *Big G Positively Cures the Worst Cases of* ———
> Wine is a mocker and strong drink is raging.
> *Victims of Secret Vice Should Try Indapo.*

While writing such as this held very small appeal for the Baptists, it was read with considerable amusement and a growing sense of respect by many men of standing in Waco.

Perhaps the most colorful of Brann's admirers was Judge George Bruce Gerald, a Mississippian who had brought his family to Waco after the war. The Judge had organized Company F, Eighteenth Mississippi Infantry, and had fought at Manassas under General Lee. He had been wounded twice in the course of the war. He was erect, tall, and slender, and in a town where violence was reasonably commonplace, the

Judge's exploits were as legendary as his reputation for a sense of honesty.

For example, he ran for county judge on the platform of cleaning up the gambling establishments of the town. Elected, he announced that all gambling establishments would cease operation immediately. When word reached the Judge that one such gathering place had failed to comply with the edict, he strode up the stairs, broke in the door, personally smashed the fixtures, threw them out the window, and published a notice in the paper threatening to repeat the performance if the proprietors should fail to heed the warning. He was appointed postmaster during the Cleveland administration, and during his term he was accidentally shot in the palm by his son, Erin, who was a spastic. Blood poisoning kept the Judge bedridden for half a year, and he was unable thereafter to move his left arm.

Brann must have heard two classic stories concerning Judge Gerald's hot temper. On one occasion a streetcar conductor failed to stop and pick up the Judge's wife, Alpha, who was waiting not far from their home on the northeast corner of Ashland and Alexander, about two miles north of central Waco. The Judge observed the slight, picked up the heavy cane he habitually carried, ran after the streetcar, and soundly caned the conductor. The fact that he was a founder of St. Paul's Episcopal Church on South Fourth Street and a member of the vestry did not prevent him from applying his cane to the rector of the church at the peak of an argument whose subject has been lost to posterity.

Although Gerald was not without enemies, his exceptional honesty was doubted in no quarter. Thus when a new courthouse was built, it was Gerald who handled the money. Eventually this same deep-rooted sense of honesty caused him to resign from St. Paul's, when a lesser man would have retained his church membership and paid lip service to the beliefs for which it stood.

There were two tragedies in the Judge's life. One was the affliction of his son, Erin. The other was that his daughter, Florence, after a proper young-lady's education at Stanton, Virginia, and Mary Baldwin, in Philadelphia, became an actress—an occupation, in those days, to bring shame to any decent family. The fact that Florence was an extremely talented actress was no concern of her father's, and his shame would not have been alleviated in the least had he known that later on Florence was to act with George Arliss and receive praise for her performances from such critics as Alexander Woollcott, Heywood Broun, Burns Mantle, and Channing Pollock. When Florence played in Waco on February 21, 1891 (as Nellie Denver in "The Silver King"), at Garland's Opera House, the doors of her home were locked to her just as securely as she was locked from her disappointed father's affections. Florence was also a poetess. In 1880 she dedicated *Adenheim and Other Poems* to her father and mother.

It is not at all improbable that Gerald, himself an iconoclast at heart, was among those present at Slattery's lecture when Brann rose up in the audience and exchanged verbal brickbats with the speaker. It was the type of incident that would have appealed immensely to a man like the Judge.

Another man who was almost certainly present at the Slattery lecture was William H. Ward, Brann's editorial associate on the *Daily News*. Ward, a huge man who had come to Waco from Corsicana, was as close a companion as Brann had in his life. Ward lived in the same boardinghouse at 809 Austin, and very soon after the Waco *Iconoclast* was born, Ward joined the staff as business manager. Having lived in Waco for a number of years, Ward was able to guide the newcomer—in so far as Brann was willing to be guided.

The Apostle was not much of a mixer. Printers who knew him when he was associated with the *Houston Post* recall that he was pretty much a lone wolf. After the day's work they often saw him stroll down Congress Avenue, a few blocks from the *Post*, to May's Saloon, where most of the *Post* workers forgathered for a beer. Brann always took a small jug along and had it filled. He never "set 'em up" for the boys nor accepted treats from them. He just drank his beer, had his jug filled, and went on to his residence at San Jacinto and Dallas streets.

Except when close to his family or to his few intimate friends, Brann was a stranger to the customary camaraderie of what we today call "outgoing people." He walked in the world of ideas, and it is fair to assume that he was so warmed by the satisfying heat of a well-turned essay, by the pleasure of plucking an appropriate metaphor startlingly out of context, that he did not need—as less creative people do—the companionship of others, either to relieve him from boredom or to buttress his sense of security as an individual.

If he had not possessed this quality of aloofness, which has frequently been a hallmark of writers who take a lonely stand, Brann would have been a jolly good fellow rather than an iconoclast. He would surely have taken one or two flings at the A.P.A. and then let the matter drop. But he was a terrier, and he reported gleefully in the June issue the jail sentence and $500 fine handed down to Warren E. Price, of San Francisco, editor of the *A.P.A. Magazine*, for sending obscene matter through the mails.

Perhaps the current campaign against salacious comic books would be more effective if more civic-inspired laments were patterned after Brann's essay on Price:

. . . Price appears to be a thrifty-minded cuss, for in addition to editing the great organ of the Apes—the sewer through which most of the bigotry and bile of those fanatics and fools pours out upon the public—he conducted a bookstore which served as a "fence" for contraband art and libidinous literature. One would suppose that such merchandise would be kept sub-rosa and displayed only to aphrodisiacal dames and habitues of the Chinese opium dens; but it developed at the trial that Price had actually sent circulars to school children, calling attention to his unequaled stock of moral corruption. And Price, be it remembered, is one of the high muck-a-mucks of those tearful patriots and pious parrots who are "rallying around the little red schoolhouse" to protect it from the corruptive influence of the Papists! "Angels and ministers of grace defend us!" Set the wolf to guard the lamb, the jackal to keep watch and ward among our sacred dead, and the Apes to protect our innocents! Nor does the attempt of Price to corrupt the school children measure the deep damnation of this moral pervert. It was proved that he had betrayed to the police other dealers in like literature that he might monopolize the sale of such filth in San Francisco. There may be truth among pirates and honor among thieves, but we look in vain for either among those legitimate descendants of Gulliver's unclean yahoos, the professional Apes. While corrupting the children Price vented his rheum upon the garments of the brides of God. Page after page of his paper was devoted to the most bestial abuse of the Roman Catholic sisterhood—to branding the inmates of convents as but little better than bawds. I am not surprised that he broke into prison. A man capable of such calumnies as he emitted month after month is equal to any crime requiring no physical courage. Instead of being incarcerated in a well-regulated penitentiary, he should have been hanged in a hair halter and his foul carcass left to fatten kites. Doubtless some honest and earnest people identify themselves with the A.P.A.—ignorance is easily misled by designing demagogues; but I have yet to learn of an Ape leader in whom a cathode ray would discover a good moral character. Warren E. Price and ex-Priest Slattery are fair samples of the fellows who make A. P. Apeism a profession and fatten at the expense of fools. Price is in a federal prison for an offense worse than murder, that of corrupting the very babes for boodle—an infamy that would crimson with shame the brazen brow of Pandarus and add new obloquy to the detested name of Tarquin. Slattery has gone, whither God only knows, and even the Devil doesn't care. He seems to have crawled off the earth after his Texas itinerary, in company with the alleged ex-nun whom he was carting around the country to pander to the prurient appetites of off-color dames by relating naughty tales of desiring nuns and accommodating priests. Slattery didn't get into the penitentiary; but he got out of Waco p. d. q.—and he'll never come back. He came as the avowed exponent of "muscular Christianity," and promised a congregation—composed chiefly of women —that he'd do something awfully dreadful to any editor who "dared assail his moral character." Then he undertook to make the same kind of play at a stag party, but didn't succeed. "His coward lips did from their color fly." He meekly took the fighting lie and canine epithet, then folded his tent like the Arab and made an inglorious sneak. The Apes must indeed be proud of their spokesman. An "American Protective Association" with Price bearing aloft its gonfalon and Slattery enunciating its principles! Think of men, born in Old Glory's sacred shadow, trailing in the wake of a brace of he-bawds who peddle obscene literature to babes and seek to corral the dirty dollar by defaming "The Angels of Buena Vista," those heroic women who are ever ready to do battle to the death with "the pestilence that walketh in darkness." Nor are these bipedal brutes, these professional panders to the prurient, these assassins of reputation, these high-binders in the world of morals, the exception to the rule—the black sheep of the A.P.A. hierarchy. Every professional exponent of A. P. Apeism is either a shameless political adventurer or graceless mountebank who's in the unclean business for boodle. Pick up any paper published in the interest of the catacombers and you'll find the same base innuendoes aimed at the sacerdotal order that has been glorified by a Pere Marquette and hallowed by a Father Damien—the same cowardly and unclean flings at consecrated women who would go to Price himself, and minister to him with more than motherly tenderness, were he stricken with the black death and deserted by those to his heart most dear. "By their fruits ye shall know them." The fruits of A. P. Apeism are hate and discord that may yet flame forth in civil strife and desolate the land. The fruits of the Catholic orders are love and charity to all, regardless of race or creed, glory or shame. Even a Slattery cannot fall so low that the Sisters of Charity would decline to succor him in his hour of distress. I am no sectarian; I care naught for the Catholic creed. Nor am I fighting the battles of the priesthood—its members are usually able to give a good account of themselves; but when men professing to be countrymen of mine—guardians of the flag of my fathers—assail with vindictive calumny women whose mission is one of mercy, I long for the power to transform the English tongue into the writhen bolts of Jove and hurl the cowardly and unclean curs to the profoundest depths of Hell.

The June issue also gives us an indication of the dim view Brann took of the writing of James Whitcomb Riley.

James Whitcomb Riley, the poetical ass with the three-story name, which he invariably inflicts upon the public in full, has broken out again. He grasps his cornstalk fiddle and twitters:

"Oh; her beautiful eyes! They are as blue as the dew
On the violet's bloom when the morning is new,
And the light of their love is the gleam of the sun
O'er the meadows of spring where the quick shadows run.
As the morn shifts the mists and the clouds from the skies—
So I stand in the dawn of her beautiful eyes."

Beautiful! Slides off slick as grease! But we are pained, Jamesie, absolutely pained to learn that "the light of their love" is intermittent. But perchance you couldn't stand to have the calcium turned on all the time. We learn from the following stanza that even a semi-occasional burst of splendor is too much for you, —causes you to wilt like turnip tops in a green-grocer's window:

"And her beautiful eyes are as midday to me,
When the lily-bell bends with the weight of the bee,
And the throat of the thrush is a-pulse in the heat,
And the senses are drugged with the subtle and sweet
And delirious breaths of the air's lullabies—
So I swoon in the noon of her beautiful eyes."

Ah, God! a little ice water and a fan, please. Chafe his throbbing temples with a Posey county corncob, and if that doesn't bring him 'round slap a "half-chawed chaw o' nateral leaf" in his left eye! Ah, that fixes him! He revives, he totters to his feet, he smites his breast, he gropes hither and yon in his delirious ecstasy. Once more he speaks, and his words are hoarse with the passion that causes him to wobble in his walk and catch his perfumed breath on the instalment plan:

> "Oh, her beautiful eyes! They have smitten mine own
> As a glory glanced down from the glare of the throne;
> And I reel, and I falter and fall as afar
> Fell the shepherds that looked on the mythical star,
> And yet dazed in the tidings that bade them arise,
> As I grope through the night of her beautiful eyes."

Well, dodgast our fool luck, he's squatted again! Stun blind and digging at the roots of the daisies with his finger nails like Romeo pawing up the pave in Friar Laurence's cell! Knocked out and completely done for by a glance from a girl who may have holes in her stockings and a hiatus in her head! Perhaps she was cross-eyed and that tangled him up. We hope the smitten Hoosier will recover the use of both legs and eyes,—that his falling sickness may not become chronic. Perhaps he can persuade his star-eyed charmer to wear green goggles or only squint at him through a piece of smoked glass. He might try splitting a thousand blackjack fence rails as a bracer. By the time he finished the task he would probably tumble to the fact that he-poets-of-passion are not in demand. Anacreon was the last one that could get the erotic jim-jams without also getting guyed. Somebody should take the whole tribe of he-warblers aside and inform them that writing poetry—even good poetry, without any love swoons in it—is devilish poor business for grown-up men. If the poetic muse will persist in haunting a fellow he is excusable for occasionally breaking into song while he draws a fat bacon rind down the shining blade of his bucksaw; but he should not get into the habit of it. When a sure-enough man cannot do anything but warble he needs medical treatment.

An attack on the A.P.A., an appraisal of Riley, a review of Tolstoy's *Kreutzer Sonata*, a defense of the Jews, and a tirade against cats were among the articles that made the June, 1895, issue of the *Iconoclast* the most successful and widely read so far.

But even while it was being circulated across newsstands and through post-office windows to an ever widening circle, an event was occurring right in Waco that was made to order for the fiery editor of the *Iconoclast*, and he was quick to seize upon it. The affair was to divide the town into fist-swinging, gun-toting factions; it would lead to the violent deaths of four human beings and would cause old men to grow choleric at the very mention of Brann's name more than five decades later.

The Crime

CHAPTER 5

The event that shocked Waco in the summer of 1895 was the seduction and impending motherhood of a student from Brazil named Antonia Teixeira. The enormity of the scandal can only be appreciated after a close look at Baylor University and its proud history.

Baylor was (and is) the educational pride and joy of every good Baptist in Texas. Owned by the Baptist General Convention of Texas, the university was founded at Independence, Texas, in 1845 by Judge R. E. B. Baylor, a native of Kentucky whose public service included a term in the United States Congress. In 1851 the Reverend Rufus C. Burleson was elected president of the school at the age of only twenty-eight. Ten years later he and his faculty moved to Waco and absorbed Waco Classical School, which became known as Waco University. In 1886, Waco University adopted the old Baylor name and became Baylor University at Waco.

The university proper was located a mile south of Waco on Fifth and Speight streets. Two large brick oblong buildings were joined at the ground floor by a glassed-in corridor, and the whole was surrounded by a wide lawn of green grass and carefully pruned hackberry and elm trees. Each of the three-story buildings had been built in a Victorian-Gothic architectural style, a curious blend of dignity in the mass and garishness in detail. The center of each building for about twenty feet, seemed to have been pushed forward a little from the rest, giving the impression of massive towers within the larger oblongs. At their tops these central towers supported little pillared porches capped by steep mansard roofs, and at the four corners of each structure were similar, smaller towers, each with its ornamental little porch and roof.

The two buildings had been built in 1886 and 1887 and included the dormitory, classrooms, assembly halls, dining hall, and kitchens. Many of the men students lived closer to town in a long ramshackle building at Fifth and Webster, which had been part of the old Waco University before it combined with Baylor. This was Maggie Houston Hall. It had two porches that stretched the whole length of the building, one above the other, and it was built entirely of wood.

The university catalogue accurately reflected Baylor, both physically and intellectually.

. . . Georgia Burleson Hall is the dormitory for young ladies. It contains 75 rooms. Boarders must bring their own bed linen, toilet articles, and such incidental room furnishings as they desire. Young ladies are also requested to bring one plate, knife, fork, and spoon. This is to prevent the taking of such utensils from the dining hall for occasional use in the rooms. . . .

. . . The Department of Moral and Mental Philosophy, logic and evidences of Christianity, conducted by Dr. Burleson. The study of philosophy and logic as taught in this department is not to familiarize the student with the learned but now exploded theories of past ages, but to prepare every student to become a true patriot and devoted Christian. . . .

. . . The primary department relies upon MacDuffy's readers, Swinton's Spellers, Maury's Geographies. . . .

. . . Music, elocution, deportment, mathematics, grammar, Latin, history of the Bible, French, German, Spanish, ancient and modern history, philosophy. . . .

. . . Three hundred and fifty-five males. . . . One hundred and ninety-seven females. . . .

. . . Parents are urged not to send sweetmeats, cakes, or other confections to the students. They need have no fear that the table set by the University is lacking either in nourishment or variety. . . .

One can imagine what Brann, a devoted classicist, thought of the curriculum. He could picture the virility that built Greece, the "exploded theories" for which men died of hemlock, lingeringly on the rack, or in flame, the great laughter of Aristophanes, Boccaccio, Rabelais, Shakespeare—he could imagine them all watered down to nothing by a fear that perhaps the "explosions" had not been as obliterating as they should have been.

And it is easier to imagine what the Baptist university authorities thought of the Apostle—a man whose mind had been twisted by the Devil, a man who took a muckraker's delight in upsetting the status quo. He was an intellectual blasphemer who quoted the Bible and coupled it with gutter slang of his own diabolical coinage. He was an evil man to whom nothing was sacred and whose peculiar delight lay in daubing the idols of civilization with foul ink brewed in his dangerous and atheistic mental workshop.

What made the news of Antonia's seduction so intriguing was not so much the fact that the wronged girl was a child but that the accused was the brother of the son-in-law of Baylor's President. The elderly President's son-in-law was the Reverend Silas Morris, owner of a print shop and editor of a Baptist monthly, *The Guardian*. It was Silas' brother, Steen Morris, whom Silas employed in his shop, that the young lady named as her assailant in court and in an interview with a reporter from the *Waco Morning News*. Both sides of the affair were meticulously reported on page 5 of the *News* on Sunday, June 16, and we can assume that the edition was sold out.

Readers of the News will remember the story of a young girl whose deplorable condition was the subject of an article in this paper some days since.

Brann's grave at Oakwood Cemetery, Waco (Note bullet mark at temple.)

Waco saloon scene typical of the 1890's

Brann (about 1892)

Dr. James D. Shaw

The Provident Building, Waco

The City Hall, Waco, in Brann's time

PRICE, 10 CENTS. $1.00 A YEAR

Brann's Iconoclast.

VOL. 7. WACO, TEXAS, U. S. A., MARCH, 1897 No. 2.

PUBLISHED MONTHLY BY W. C. BRANN.

Entered at the Postoffice, Waco, Texas, as second-class matter.

Remit by Bank Draft, P. O. or Express Money Order.
All Subscriptions Payable invariably in Advance.
The Iconoclast has no "Exchange" or free list.

OFFICE:—Rooms 32 and 33 Provident Building.

MAKE A DOLLAR

By sending four cash subscribers to the ICONOCLAST. Local
Agents wanted throughout the United States and Canada.
All postmasters and newsdealers are authorized to receive
subscriptions.

BRADLEY-MARTIN BAL-MASQUE

"Apres Moi le Deluge!"

MRS. BRADLEY-MARTIN'S sartorial kings and pseudo-queens, her dukes and DuBarrys, princes and Pompadours, have strutted their brief hour upon the mimic stage, disappearing at daybreak like foul night-birds or an unclean dream—have come and gone like the rank eructation of some crapulous Sodom, a malodor from the cloacæ of ancient capitals, a breath blown from the festering lips of half-forgotten harlots, a stench from the sepulchre of centuries devoid of shame. Uncle Sam may now proceed to fumigate himself after his enforced association with royal bummers and brazen bawds; may comb the Bradley-Martin itch bacteria out of his beard and consider, for the ten-thousandth time, the probable result of his strange commingling of royalty-worshipping millionaires and sansculottic mendicants—how best to put a ring in the nose of the golden calf ere it become a Phalaris bull and relegate him to its belly. Countless columns have been written, printed, possibly read, anent the Bradley-Martin ball—all the preachers and teachers, editors and other able idiots pouring forth voluminous opinions. A tidal wave of printer's ink has swept across the continent, churned to atoms foam by hurricanes of lawless gibberish and wild gusts of resounding gab. The empyrean has been ripped and the tympana of the too-patient gods ravished with fulsome commendation and foolish curse, showers of Parthian arrows and wholesale consignments of soft-soap darkening the sun as they hurtled hither and yon through the shrinking atmosphere. A man dropping suddenly in from Mars with a Nicaraguan canal scheme for the consideration of Uncle Sam, would have supposed this simian hubbub and auscrise todo meant nothing less than a new epocha for the universe, it being undecided whether it should be auriferous or argentiferous—an age of gold or a cycle of silver. Now that the costly "function" has linked itself into a howling farce, an uncomfortable failure, and the infuscated revellers recovered somewhat from royal katzenjammer, we find

that the majestic earth has not moved an inch out of its accustomed orbit, that the grass still grows and the cows yet calve—that the law of gravitation remains unrepealed, and Omnipotence continues to bring forth Mazzaroth in his season and guide Arcturus with his sons. Perchance in time the American people may become ashamed of having been thrown into a panic by the painful effort of a pudgy parvenu to outdo even the Vanderbilts in ostentatious vulgarity. Rev. Billy Kersands Rainsford cannot save this country with his mouth, nor can Mrs. Bradley-Martin wreck it with her money. It is entirely too large to be permanently affected by the folly of any one fool. Preacher and parvenu were alike making a grand-stand play. Now that the world has observed them, and not without interest, let us hope that they will subside for a little season.

This Dame DuBarry extravaganza was not without significance to those familiar with history and its penchant for repetition; but was by no means an epoch-maker. It was simply one more festering sore on the syphilitic body social—another unclean maggot industriously wriggling in the malodorous carcass of a canine. It was another evidence that civilization is in a continual flux, flowing now forward, now backward—a brutal confession that the new world aristocracy is oozing at present thro' the Armida-palace or Domdaniel of DuBarrydom. The Bradley-Martins are henceforth entitled to wear their ears interlaced with laurel leaves as sign of superiority in their "set." They won the burro pennant honestly, if not, easily, daylight being plainly visible between their foam-crested cruppers and the panting nostrils of the Vanderbilts. They are now monarchs of Rag-fair, chief gyasticuti of the boundless realm of Nescience and Noodledom. Mrs. Bradley-Martin has triumphed gloriously, raised herself by her own garters to the vulgar throne of Vanity, the dais of the almighty dollar. She is now Delphic oracle of doodle-bugs and hierophant of the hot stuff. *Viva Regina!* Likewise, rats! Like most of New York's aristocracy, she is of even nobler lineage than Lady Vere de Vere, daughter of an hundred earls, having been sired by a duly registered American sovereign early in the present century. His coat-of-arms was a cooper's adz rampant, a beer-barrel couchant and the motto, "Two heads are better than one." By wearing his neighbors' cast clothes and feeding his family on cornbread and "sow-belly," he was able to lay the foundation of that fortune which has made his daughter *facile princeps* of New York's patricians. John Jacob Astor, who acted as royal consort to the cooper's regal daughter in the *quadrille d' honneur*, is likewise descended from noble Knights (of Labor) and dames of high degree. He traces his lineage in an unbroken line to that haughty Johann Jakob who came to America in the steerage, wearing a Limburger linsey-woolsey and a pair of wooden shoes. Beginning life in the new world as a rat-catcher, he

Brann's Iconoclast

69

Brann (probably 1896)

"An Intellectual Cocktail."

**THE ONLY AMERICAN MAGAZINE
THAT EVER SECURED 100,000
READERS IN A SINGLE YEAR.**

Published Monthly at Waco, Texas.

$1 a Year.   10 Cents a Number.

Leading Newsdealers Everywhere.

"It Strikes To Kill."

Full-page advertisement for the *Iconoclast* from *Brann's Annual*, 1895

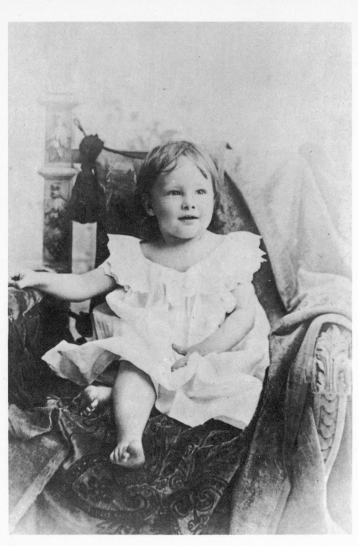

Brann's son, Billy (about 1892)

Brann's daughter, Gracie (about 1897)

Brann's home in Waco, "The Oaks"

Judge George Bruce Gerald

EXTRA.

Waco Daily Telephone.

WACO, TEXAS, FRIDAY NIGHT, NOV. 19, 1897.

GERALD - HARRIS STREET DUEL.

Three men Engaged in Deadly Combat on Austin Avenue.

W. A. HARRIS WAS KILLED

J. W. Harris was Mortally Wounded and G. B. Gerald Has two Wounds---J. W. Harris Fired the First Shot.

At a time when the streets of Waco were crowded with men, women and children, this afternoon, a street duel participated in by three persons occurred on the most prominent business corner of this city, during which many shots were exchanged. One was killed and two ....

W. A. Harris, was across the street near the Citizens' National bank.

Judge Gerald crossed the intersection of the two streets and the firing began. The first shot came from the pistol of J. W. Harris and two were fired before Judge Gerald drew his pistol ... fire and wa...

ner Drug Store d was near me. out of the way. I shooting' I ste walked away H the first ball gr head. As I walke crossing the stree crossing the stre

"Who shot firs'

"J. W. Harri' twice before Ge

Judge Gerald tacked front an Harris fired fir to defend himse at J. W. Harris hi mfrom the r to turn on hin

Judge Gerald corpse to W. A. "The cowards hind. They in the open."

The affair h of excitement the men has n when the rep heard every ris and Ger

W. S. Jar shot in th ing the (

One pers "I was sta zens' Nation the street t Store and was about Harris we Old Corn leaning u Gerald wa the two fa shooting. I another man, Harris, who at Gerald and ly the pistol by a policen the street te he had reach Harris ha I was on top o had got over hi Then a policen o strugg

Headline on the Gerald-Harris shooting, *Waco Daily Telephone*, November 19, 1897

76

Intersection of Fourth and Austin where the Gerald-Harris
duel occurred

Headline on the Brann-Davis shooting, *Dallas Semi-Weekly News*, April 5, 1898

The details of this case were brought to light yesterday by official investigation, resulting in the arrest of H. S. (Stein) [Steen] Morris on a charge of rape, alleged to have been committed on the person of the complainant, Antonio [Antonia] Teixeira.

This was followed by the arrest of Morris, who was taken into custody by officers Torrance and Barnard on a warrant issued by Justice Earle, and committed to jail, but was subsequently released on bail in the sum of $3,000, his bond being signed by Messrs. F. B. Williams, J. T. Battle, O. I. Holbert, Bart Moore, and E. E. Easterling.

The complainant, Antonio Teixeira, is in her sixteenth year, is a native of Bihia [Bahia], Brazil, and came to this country in 1892 to be educated for missionary work in Brazil. For this purpose the girl was put to school in Baylor College, this city.

During the first year her tuition was paid and she attended school as a boarder. Subsequently board, tuition and clothes were furnished by Dr. Burleson, and the girl assisted Mrs. Burleson in her household duties, attending school during certain hours of the day.

The story of the girl's condition and trouble is best told by the statements of herself and others connected, directly, and indirectly, with the deplorable affair which culminated in the arrest of Morris on the most heinous of charges yesterday.

THE GIRL'S STORY

A news reporter saw the girl at the residence of Mr. and Mrs. O. W. Jenkins, and received from her the following story of her history since landing in this country, together with a statement of her condition and its cause. She said:

"In January, 1892, I landed in New York in company with Rev. Z. C. Taylor and family and went from thence to Philadelphia, where Mrs. Taylor was the subject of a surgical operation. I accompanied Mr. Taylor and the children to Belton, Texas, to the home of Mrs. Taylor's parents.

"From Belton I came to Waco in July, 1892, and entered Baylor University, taking up my abode with the president, Dr. Burleson and his wife. Mr. Taylor had promised me five years of schooling, etc., to fit me for missionary service on my return home.

"My father was at one time a Catholic priest, but was converted by a Baptist missionary and became a minister of that church before his death, which occurred eight years ago, my mother and five children surviving him.

"Stein Morris took his meals at the Burleson residence during the greater portion of my stay there, rooming in another house in the same yard. He always treated me with great freedom, taking certain liberties when we were alone, but ignored me when others were present.

"He, Morris, often entreated me to come to his room, and asked me to meet him at the barn, but I did not like him and was always afraid of him, hence did not go.

"The occasion of his first assault upon my person was in the early days of November, 1894, between 8:00 and 9:00 o'clock at night. He came to the kitchen door and asked me if I did not want something good to drink. He then opened the door, took me by the arm and forcibly drew me out into the yard. He had some whitish looking liquor in a bottle which he offered me to drink. I said I did not want it, but was induced by him to drink. I do not know what it was, the liquor tasted sweet.

"Whatever it was, the liquor affected me so that I became dizzy. He then threw me to the ground and took liberties with my person. I was held so closely by him that I could not utter a cry. On this occasion he let me go after a few moments, without fully accomplishing his purpose. At the time of this assault I was alone in the house with Grandma Jenkins, who is 83 years old. I was not very badly injured by Morris on this occasion and was able to attend school the next day.

"The morning following the first assault I spoke to Mrs. Burleson and told her that Mr. Morris had been bothering me, but did not tell her what he had done. Mrs. Burleson repeated my statement to Mrs. S. L. Morris, Stein's sister-in-law, who spoke to Stein Morris about it and he denied having seen me at all on the occasion. It was some weeks later, November 20, I think, he accosted me the second time at about the same hour of the evening. I shut the door on him but he pushed it open, took hold of me and dragged me out as before.

"After getting me out in the yard he repeated his treatment of me, on the former occasion. But this time he was frightened away by a noise as of someone approaching. I again spoke to Mrs. Burleson that he kept after me and she again spoke to Mrs. Morris, but nothing was done.

"The last of November Stein Morris made his third and last assault upon me and in practically the same manner and at the same hour as before. This time he accomplished his purpose. The next day I was unable to attend school, owing to my injuries, he having lacerated me badly.

"I said nothing of this last assault to anyone, as before my statements were denied by Morris and disbelieved by the others.

"On or about December 1st Mr. Morris went to Louisiana, and three weeks later returned with a bride. I was glad that he was married and said so, because I thought I would escape further ill usage at his hands. Knowledge of my condition was first gained in the Burleson household some months after I, myself, had discovered that I was enceinte. It was at first suspected from certain evidence and a physician called in who confirmed the fact.

"The above confirmation came four and one-half months after pregnancy. I was then removed to the home of Mrs. O. W. Jenkins, whose husband is a nephew of Mrs. Dr. Burleson. I have been here since April and have only left the premises once, that being to appear in court today.

"Yes, I was kindly treated by Mrs. Burleson and all the family, but, of course, I assisted in the household work.

"No, I did not prefer any charge against Stein Morris until brought into court on a subpoena from the Justice. There I made the same statement that I am making now and the same I made to you a week or ten days ago, when you first interviewed me for the News, only you did not ask me and I did not tell you how my ruin was accomplished.

"I have been kindly treated, indeed by Mrs. Jenkins, who has done all that a mother could have done for me, and I shall remain with her as long as I am permitted, because I shall never feel as though I could face my own mother again, after this."

DR. BURLESON INTERVIEWED

In view of the connection, indirectly, of Dr. Burleson and his college with this unfortunate affair, he was called upon by a news reporter last evening and asked for a statement, so far as he knew, of the girl, her actions, and general deportment during her residence with his family, as well as of her trouble, which he gave as follows:

"At the request of Reverend Z. C. Taylor, himself an old student and his wife a distant relative of our family, I took the Brazilian girl Antonio Teixeira to board and school.

"It was the earnest desire of both Mrs. Burleson and myself to prepare her for missionary work in her native land and it is with exceeding great reluctance that I say aught to reflect on the character of this most unfortunate girl nor would I now do so but that the sternest necessity of justice demands it at my hands.

"The statement, which has been made, that the girl was treated as a servant and not given money compensation, is utterly false. She assisted my wife and daughter in their household duties as any member of the family might have done in her place.

"In fact the girl was in all respects treated as my granddaughter. In return for her assistance I gave her board, tuition and clothes or more than double the worth of her help.

"After she had been in my house several months I was deeply pained to learn that, with all her genial nature and pleasing disposition, the girl was utterly untrustworthy, in fact could not be trusted at all, and my wife was even forced to keep her household expense money under lock and key on this account. In addition to the other faults, the girl was crazy after the boys.

"As to the statement that the girl ever informed Mrs. Burleson of an assault upon her by Stein Morris or any other person it is wholly false. On the contrary she stated to Mrs. Burleson on two different occasions that she would swear on the Bible that no man ever touched her in that way.

"On account of these faults and failings we admonished her, prayed for her and wept over her. She would promise to reform but seemed powerless to resist these inherent passions and vices.

"Finding our efforts vain we tried to get her back to Brazil, but failed. Being too honest to impose her upon unsuspecting people and too kindly inclined to set her adrift while hope remained, we kept her.

"There were, at one time, shameful rumors about her and a young student at the University. When arraigned as to their truth, he pleaded that she forced herself upon him. With all these mournful facts before me I think the idea of rape in this case simply preposterous."

STEEN MORRIS TALKS

Steen Morris, the man who stands charged with a heinous offense, alleged to have been committed on the person of Antonia Teixeira, was visited by a news reporter, while occupying a cell in the County Jail yesterday afternoon.

Morris took his arrest and incarceration fairly well

and seemed to bear up under the awful charge against him better than might have been expected.

When asked as to his guilt or innocence of the charge he said:

"I'm entirely innocent of the crime charged against me and will prove it whenever the opportunity is given me."

"Do you deny responsibility for the girl's condition?" asked the reporter.

"Yes sir. I deny any kind or character of intimacy with the girl, having never had aught to do with her in that way."

"What is your occupation, Mr. Morris?" was the next question asked.

"I'm a printer by trade and am employed in the office of my brother, Reverend S. L. Morris, in this city."

This closed the interview with Mr. Morris, who is a young man with little to distinguish him from his fellows. He converses intelligently and spoke of his troubles freely. He has a charming wife to whom he was married in December of last year, at her home in Louisiana.

These are the full facts in the matter from all sides and the News leaves its readers and the public to judge of them as they may incline.

At the time this matter was brought out in the News it was understood that the same would be investigated and properly sifted. Now that same has been brought into court, we will give all facts bearing thereon in our possession.

As to the unfortunate girl, it is understood that a

move will be made among the citizens to raise all money necessary with which to keep and properly care for her until she shall have regained health and strength and become better able to care for herself.

It is indeed a sad story and one which all could wish there was no necessity for relating.

There appears to be some difference of opinion among the physicians who made the examination, arising, perhaps, from the different manner in which same was made.

The statement of the girl as to the laceration of her person, however, is borne out by competent medical authority.

At 5:00 A.M. on June 17 Antonia was delivered of a baby girl by Dr. C. T. Young at the Jenkins home, 908 South Ninth Street. The baby was white, which dispelled the most vicious of the rumors being circulated by Steen's adherents.

The *Morning News* of Wednesday, June 18, reported:

Another chapter has been added to the sensational legal drama in which Antonia Teixeira and Steen Morris are the principal actors.

The new element was introduced in the shape of a tiny stranger, who made her arrival at the home of Mr. and Mrs. O. W. Jenkins in the early hours of yesterday morning.

The infant, a miniature edition of the mother, was born to Antonia Teixeira at 5:00 o'clock A.M., Dr. C. T. Young being the physician in attendance. The child is one of the tiniest specimens of the human family, being to babyhood what the mother is to womanhood.

Despite its size the child, a girl, she is fairly well developed and gives promise of continued existence. The mother is progressing better than might have been expected and she too has a fair chance of recovery.

A rumor was current yesterday morning that the mother was sinking fast and could not survive through the day. This report coming to the ear of Justice Earle he repaired at once to the Jenkins residence for the purpose of obtaining an anti mortem statement from the patient.

On arrival, however, the Justice learned that both mother and child were resting easily and neither in any immediate danger.

The birth of a child to Antonia Teixeira has had the effect of rekindling the flame of curious speculation concerning herself and the man at whose door she lays the burden of an awful crime.

Every care and attention necessary to one in her trying condition will be secured to the helpless girl, who by reason of motherhood is doubly an object of commiseration. The best of medical aid has been secured.

The hearing of the case against Morris, on examining trial will necessarily be postponed on account of the complainant's condition, and the case re-set for preliminary examination to some more convenient time.

Zealously anxious to show its nonpartisanship, the *News* had a reporter track down another rumor—that a serving girl named Maggie Bettinger employed in the Morris home had abruptly left after a similar encounter with young Steen. Maggie was not available for comment. She was visiting relatives, her father explained, and was not well. But there had been never any trouble with Steen Morris. It was one of young Morris' friends—a boy named Jones. No, the initials he could not recall, nor the lad's home. He was simply a visitor passing through town.

The *News* reported the interview in detail on Thursday, and the aura of gratification at laying a rumor to rest was almost as thick as the circulation figures.

Thanks to thorough newspaper coverage of the case, Waco had never been so upwrought in its forty-year history. Every small bit of gossip added fuel to the fires of debate and partisanship.

The parents of Baylor students, the stanch Baptists, and those who sought to profit by aligning themselves with them formed a faction whose goal was to deplore the whole affair, to minimize it, and to defame the girl's character. The sincerely outraged citizens found themselves the unwilling allies of the lascivious, the sensation-seekers, and the elements who watched with glee the discomfiture of an ultrarighteous group trying to euphemize a torrid scandal.

Groups of men gathered on the street corners, in hotel lobbies, and on the courthouse lawn. Farmers in town for the day were told the story in versions limited only by the imaginations of the raconteurs.

Youngsters heard the tale from their older brothers, and Baylor students who had studied with Antonia became celebrities.

For a crusading journalist like Brann, the case was made to order. It was a scandal that encompassed—in his view—all the derelictions and vicious hypocrisies he had been holding up to the Baptists in his *Iconoclast* and in his earlier newspaper editorials.

It would be gilding the lily with a whitewash brush to say that Brann was not well aware of the circulation value of a full-throated attack on Baylor. But it would be equally absurd to dismiss his consistent record of idol-smashing and expect him to overlook the matter entirely. His written record paints him a man of sensitiveness, idealism, and of that tremendous indignation common to most prophets and standard-bearers of morality. The fact that he was outspoken, usually with very unpleasant consequences, argues that he was certainly moved as much by conviction as by expediency. A more docile man would long since have embraced a less contentious life—particularly when contention had brought him neither security nor peace of mind, and his voluminously recorded moral and religious views are convincing proof that Brann's labors sprang from a firm base of sincerity and fundamental honesty.

In the July *Iconoclast* Brann set in motion the events that were to result in the violent deaths of four men. He wrote:

The *Iconoclast* is not in the habit of commenting on particular social ulcers and special sectarian scandals. It prefers to deal with broad principles rather than individual offenders. To even catalogue the sexual crimes of professing Christians and people of social preeminence—to turn the calcium for even a moment into all the grewsome closets of "respectability" and upon every sectarian cesspool redolent with the "odor of sanctity"—would consume the space of such a periodical, while proving about as profitable as pointing out each festering pustule on the person of a Hot Springs habitue trailing blindly in the wake of the Pandemian Venus; but once or twice in a decade a case arises so horrible in conception, so iniquitous in outline, so damnable in detail that it were impossible to altogether ignore it. Such a case has just come to light, involving Baylor University, that Bulwark of the Baptist church. I fain would pass it by, knowing as I do that criticism, however dispassionate and just, will be misconstrued by those good Baptist brethren who tried to muzzle me while ex-Priest Slattery foully defamed me, and whose religion teaches them that "with what judgment ye judge ye shall be judged; and with what measure ye mete it shall be measured to you again." But on this point they have naught to fear. Had they, for every sneaking lie they have told about me, spawned a thousand; and had "Brother" Slattery, in the fullness of his Baptist Charity, branded me as a horse-thief and proved it, I could not, though vindictive as Thersites and gifted with the vocabulary of a Carlyle, do even and exact justice to the case of Antonia Teixeira. Crimes similar in some respects have been committed in White Chapel and on Boiler avenue; but, to borrow from Macaulay, "When we put everything together—sensuality, poltroonery, baseness, effrontery, mendacity, barbarity—the result is something which in a novel we should condemn as caricature, and to which, we venture to say, no parallel can be found in history." It is a case wherein "the qualities which are the proper objects of contempt," preserve an exquisite and absolute harmony. Three times I have essayed to write of this enormous iniquity, this subter-brutish crime against the chastity of childhood, and thrice I have laid down my pencil in despair. As there is a depth of the sea to which the plummet will not descend, so are there depths of human depravity which mind cannot measure. Language hath its limits, and even a Dante could only liken the horrors of Hell to earthly symbols. It were as impossible to describe in print the case of Antonia Teixeira as to etch a discord or paint a stench. Before justice can be done to such a subject a new language must be invented—a language whose words are coals of juniper-wood, whose sentences are woven with a warp of aspics' fangs and a woof of fire.

We all remember the coming to Texas of Antonia Teixeira, the dove-eyed heteroscian, and the brass-band display made of the modest little thing by the Baptist brethren, whose long years of missionary labor in Brazil had snatched her from the Papal power—a veritable brand from the burning. A tardy consent had been wrung from her widowed mother that Antonia should be brought to Texas. The child was to be given five years' schooling, then returned to her native land to point out to her benighted Catholic countrymen the water route to the Celestial City. Relying upon this promise, the simple Brazilian woman consigned her

91

little wild-flower to the bosom of the Baptist church. Five years! What an eternity! How they would miss her at home—how they would count the days until she returned to them, a cultured lady, as wise even as the strange priests who spoke the English tongue! It must be for the best, she thought; so the poor woman crushed her heart in the name of Christ and took up her cross. And Antonia? How bright the world before her! To be educated, and useful and honored both in this world and the world to come, instead of an ignorant little beggar about the streets of Bahia. Bearded men prayed over her and sentimental women wept to know that she was saved—saved from the purgatorium of Popery! And then she was "consecrated" and began her studies at Baylor, the duly ordained "ward of the Baptist church." Not yet 13 years old, and such honors paid her—what might she not expect in the years to be? How the poor little heart must have swelled with gratitude to the good Baptist brethren, and how she must have loved everything, animate and inanimate, that the good God had made. But ere long she found herself in Dr. Burleson's kitchen instead of the class-room. Instead of digging Greek roots she was studying the esculent tuber. Instead of being prepared for missionary work, this "ward of the Baptist church" was learning the duties of the scullion—and Dr. Burleson has informed the world through the public prints that as a servant she was not worth her board and clothes. But then she was not brought hither to sling pots, but to prepare for the saving of souls. Surely the blessed Baptist church will provide its little "ward" the board and clothes. Perhaps the poor child thought that scrubbing floors and playing under-servant was part of a liberal education, for she made no complaint to her self-constituted guardians. After some three years of the kitchen curriculum she was examined in the office of a secular official and it was there found that she had not made much progress toward effective missionary work. She had heard something of the Protestant faith and salvation by water, but did not understand it. And in two years more her "education" would be complete—the promise made to her mother redeemed! But suddenly it was discovered that the "ward of the Baptist church" was about to give birth to a babe. Day by day this mournful fact became more in evidence, and finally her dish-rag and scrub-broom studies were suspended because of a press of more important business. She was sneaked off to a private house and nothing said about her condition to the secular authorities—no steps taken to bring the destroyer of this child in short dresses to justice. But the meddlesome officials concluded to look after the "ward of the Baptist church" a little, and the poor child told them, reluctantly enough, how she had been dragged from her culinary class-room, drugged and three times criminally assaulted—how she complained, "but nothing was done about it." A medical examination demonstrated conclusively that she had been the victim of foul play. What did the aged president of Baylor, that sanctum sanctorum of the Baptist church, do about it? Did he assist in bringing to justice the man who had dared invade the sanctity of his household and despoil the duly ordained "ward of the Baptist church?" Not exactly. He rushed into print with a statement to the effect that the child was a thief and "crazy after the boys"—that he had "prayed and wept over her" without avail. Are prayers and tears the only safeguards thrown around fourteen-year-old girls at Baylor? They do those things differently in Convent schools—supplement prayers and tears with a watchful care that makes illicit intercourse practically impossible. No matter how "crazy after the boys" a girl in short dresses may be, she is not permitted to go headlong to the Devil—to be torn to pieces and impregnated by some lousy and lecherous male mastodon. Dr. Burleson considered the idea that Antonia had been ravished as ridiculous, yet the doctors declare it one of the most damnable cases of outrage and laceration within their knowledge—and in matters of this kind a wicked and perverse generation is more likely to believe doctors of medicine than doctors of divinity. The students at Baylor declare that instead of being "crazy after the boys" Antonia was particularly modest and womanly. But had she been the brazen little thing which Dr. Burleson hastened to brand her, what were his duties in the premises: to guard her, with especial care, or give the "boys" an opportunity to work their will, then turn her out with a Baptist bastard at the half-developed breast? Enceinte at 14, among strangers who had promised her mother that no harm should befall her. A mother while still in short dresses, and branded in the public prints as a bawd by people who worship One who forgave Mary Magdalen! We might have expected the very devils in hell to weep for the pity of it, but "Christian charity" had not yet reached its ultima thule. Another Baptist reverend had to have his say. He was somewhat interested in the matter, his brother having been named by Antonia as her ravisher. This reverend gentleman tried to make it appear that the father of her unborn child was a negro servant and her accepted paramour. Had this been true, what an "ad." for Baylor University—that fourteen-years-old girls committed to its care conceived children by coons! But even Baylor did not deserve the terrible censure of Dr. Burleson's pious son-in-law, and Antonia replied to this insult added to injury by putting a white child in evidence—a child with the pale blue eyes and wooden face characteristic of those who defamed her. When the girl's condition became known the men about town —"publicans and sinners" such as Christ sat with, preferring their society to that of the pharisees—raised a handsome purse to provide for her and the young Baptist she was about to bring into the world, while those who should have guarded and protected her were resorting to every artifice human ingenuity could devise to blacken her name, to forestall pity, prevent charity and make an impartial trial of the case impossible. While men who never professed religion, who never expect to wear feathers and fly through Elysian fields, could not talk to each other about the case without crying, those wearing God's livery were eager to trample her down to the deepest hell to preserve the credit of their denomination. If there is anything on earth calculated to make a public prostitute of an unfortunate girl it is the treatment the Baptist brethren have accorded Antonia Teixeira.

At this writing (June 27) the preliminary trial awaits the convalescence of the child mother. I would not prejudge the case. I know not who is the guilty man; but I do know that this child was brought from a faraway home by men who promised to protect her and transform her into a cultured and useful woman, and who so far neglected their duty that she was debauched at Baylor University and her young life forever blighted. Better a thousand times that she should have remained in Brazil to say her pater nosters in the Portuguese tongue; better that she should have wedded a water-carrier in her native land and reared up sturdy sons and daughters of the Church of Rome, than to have been transported to Texas to breed illegitimate Baptists. I do know that at the very time "Brother" Slattery was warning us against the awful dangers of convent schools—and impeaching the chastity of the Catholic sisterhoods—and the Waco Baptists were crying "awmen"—this fourteen-year-old girl was growing great with child at Baylor University! I do know that while we were being assured that among all the nuns there was not one educated woman—not one competent to superintend the education of a child—a girl was completing her third year in the greatest educational institute the Baptists of Texas can boast, and in all that time she had learned but little, and that little she could have acquired almost as well in "Hell's Half-Acre." I do know that Antonia is not the first young girl to be sent from Baylor in disgrace—that she is not the first to complain of criminal assault within its sanctified walls. I do know that should a girl meet with a mishap at a convent school the Catholic priests would not turn against her and insult her family and her race by trying to fasten the fatherhood of her unborn babe upon a negro servant. I do know that instead of trying to drive the unfortunate girl to the "Reservation" with cowardly calumnies, they would draw around her the sacred circle of the Church of Rome, and if there remained within her heart one spark of noble womanhood it would be fanned by the white wings of love and charity into ethereal flame. I do know that if Antonia Teixeira was a Catholic instead of a half-baked Baptist, every man within that church would be her brother, every woman her sister,—that every church bearing the cross would be her house of refuge. I do know that so far as Baylor University is concerned the day of its destiny is over and the star of its fate hath declined; that the brutal treatment the Brazilian child received at its hands will pass into history as the colossal crime of the age, and that generations yet to be will couple its name with curses deep as those which Roman matrons heaped on the head of Sextus Tarquinius—"he that wrought the deed of shame."

The Defense

CHAPTER 6

The widely respected seventy-two-year-old President of Baylor conferred long and late with the trustees, one of whom—John T. Battle— had paid for Antonia's tuition her first year. It was not the sort of scandal that would die out if ignored—not with Brann's poised pen ready to stir the waters if they became too stagnant for the appetites of his readers.

So on August 20 Dr. Burleson published Baylor's side of the affair in a four-page brochure entitled "Baylor University and the Brazilian Girl."

Nothing grieves my heart more than to publish or even say anything disparaging a student, and especially one for whom my wife has given three years of earnest toil, tender watch care and at least $320.00 in board, tuition, books and clothing. All without a single hope of fee or reward except the joy of lifting up the lowly and educating the orphan child of a Baptist Missionary who died in a foreign land. Yet it is painfully evident that since Judge Goodrich so wisely decided the infamous charges against Steen Morris for raping the Brazilian girl utterly groundless and without a particle of evidence, and dismissed the case, persecutors of Steen Morris have redoubled their diligence in scattering vile slander over the state, especially among Baylor University patrons, American and foreign, endeavoring to show that Baylor University is an unsafe place to educate students especially females. They are portraying the Brazilian girl as a little Missionary angel, whom we degraded as a cook, and carelessly permitted her to be ruined. They have even boasted "that Baylor University is dead and that the 273,000 Baptists of Texas are disgraced forever." While all well informed people know these things to be utterly false, and gotten up by the rabble and "lewd" fellows of the baser sort, yet lest honest people may be misled, especially as we blush to hear the agents of other colleges are slyly and secretly aiding these mud slingers, I will give a brief statement of facts. First, the Brazilian girl was never "the ward of Baylor University or the Baptists of Texas." She never was a "boarder in Georgia Burleson Hall," the female boarding department of Baylor University. No one ever paid a cent on her expenses, except Capt. J. T. Battle, who seeing our heavy burden paid her tuition one year. Mrs. Burleson and I are the only persons that ever assumed any responsibility, or paid any money and all the blame, if there be any, rests on us. And how utterly blameless we are, "let facts be submitted to a candid world," facts that will stand the test of the Judgment Day.

Three years ago, in 1892, Rev. Z. C. Taylor, a be-

99

loved graduate of Baylor University and for years an efficient Missionary of Brazil, who married a relation of mine, wrote me to know what provisions Baylor University could make to educate a Brazilian girl, a daughter of the converted Catholic Priest, Teixeira, who became a Baptist preacher and after years of successful Missionary work died, leaving a large and helpless family. I replied: "Baylor University has no endowment fund, and gives free tuition to all young preachers and minor children of Texas Pastors, and has declined to do anything more, but Mrs. Burleson and I will take her in our family and furnish her board, tuition, books and clothing, and teach her housekeeping, as requested, on Saturdays, mornings, evenings when not conflicting with her studies, and all the reward that we would ask was that the girl would become as useful in the cause of religion and education in Brazil, as Miss Julia Flores, whom we educated years ago, had become in Mexico." Brother Taylor replied: "No arrangement on Earth could please me better, and I will bring her and also a young Brazilian preacher with me when I bring my wife for medical treatment to the United States." Brother Taylor reached Waco about the time that the Texas Baptist Convention was in session, in Waco, and in his great speech before that body on the Brazilian Mission, he asked permission to bring the young preacher, Geronymo Souza and the Brazilian girl to the platform and have them repeat the Lord's prayer and sing a song in the Portuguese language. This simple service, our mud slingers have magnified into "A grand ovation and public adoption of the Brazilian girl as a daughter of the Texas Baptists." Brother Taylor privately told us tenderly and frankly, "The

100

three besetting sins of the Brazilians are lust, a want of veracity and honesty." "These sad points you will have to guard in Antonio." Through him we explained to her that "She was not to be a hireling nor a servant, but a member of our family and as a daughter, and that we would endeavor to be to her a father and mother." She at once called me Grand-pa and my wife "Mamie" just as our own Grand-children do. She slept in our best room with Mrs. Jenkins my wife's Mother and had a seat given her at the table, but she preferred to wait and talk with the servants, as her Pastor, John The Baptist, who baptised her was a negro preacher. She was exceedingly kind to children, was fond of music, but loathed study and all kinds of work. And all the services she rendered over and above the trouble and annoyance of teaching her what to do and seeing that she did it, would have been dear at $1.00 per month. I committed her to Miss Emma Culbertson our primary teacher, one of the most faithful teachers Texas ever knew. She dressed as our grand-children and other students did and always rode to the University with me and my granddaughter in the buggy when it was cold, raining or muddy. No daughter was ever treated more kindly. We thought of her as the orphan daughter of a Baptist preacher who had died five thousand miles away. But alas, in less than one year, her three great national besetting sins began to crop out fearfully. Mrs. Burleson and her noble christian teacher admonished and warned her in vain. She was clearly detected in the school-room of stealing a fine gold pen and also in stealing articles of clothing at home. Her want of truthfulness and passion for boys were equally appalling. And she seemed to have no conception of the enormity of the crimes of lying, lust and stealing. When we saw these master passions burning in her bones, we knew all tears, entreaties, money and prayers were utterly wasted. We wrote to Brother Taylor we could do nothing with her, and asked to send her back to Brazil just as early as possible, as she was liable to disgrace herself, and we did not want such a shame in our family nor on a student in Baylor University. We give these painful facts to show how false are the statements, that when she came she was a beautiful innocent girl, almost an angel.

Mrs. Burleson tried to get a noble christian Missionary returning to Brazil to take her, but she said: "I would do anything on earth to relieve you and Dr. Burleson of your burden, but I know her and cannot allow her to associate with my daughters on shipboard." As we could not send her to Brazil we gave her closer attention than we ever gave to any ten girls in Baylor University during the last forty-four years. The only way we could have guarded her more closely would have been to chain her in a cell with iron bars. When Mrs. Burleson sent her on an errand to a near neighbor's house, she would feign some excuse to go two or three blocks beyond, where there was a boy with whom she could laugh and talk. And when requested to come home directly after school was dismissed, she would slip around to some house where there were boys and then say: "Miss Emma kept me after school." Miss Emma detected her in writing a note to a boy saying: "Meet me at the Pecan tree on Waco Creek this evening." Her conduct caused shameful talk among the boys, as all students who know the facts will testify. Some weeks before her disgrace was established, Mrs.

Burleson was warning her with tears, when Antonio "The Little Angel" replied solemnly: "Why Mamie I am ashamed for you to suspect me. I will lay my hand on this Bible and swear that no man ever touched me" yet on her single testimony an honorable young man was thrown into jail, and his young wife, and aged parents and family made inexpressibly miserable. As soon as Dr. Halbert examined her and pronounced her disgraced, Mrs. Burleson went to bed sick and has never been perfectly well since, though she can call God to witness that she did everything in her power to save the girl. We immediately wrote to Galveston, Dallas and Ft. Worth to find some safe Reformatory where she could be placed, but Mrs. Burleson felt reluctant to put her among entire strangers, and it was suggested that as Mrs. Ollie Jenkins had no children, and had some skill in reforming "fallen women" she might take her, which she consented to do free of all charge. Dr. Halbert, our family physician, kindly consented to give her all necessary medical attention free of all charge. These facts will demonstrate how malicious and black are the falsehoods sent broad-cast over Texas: first; that Baylor University and the Baptists were ever responsible for this unfortunate girl, and second how equally black and damnable are the lies that Mrs. Burleson and I made her a cook, and cast her off in the kitchen to be ruined and then thrust her into the streets to be picked up by Catholics and other "publicans and sinners." I learned from my Welsh ancestors and my Father that "Next to God every man should worship his wife, his mother and his daughter, and should be ever ready to defend a woman's honor with his life's blood"; and there never was a time when

I would not have slain any man if I found him outraging a woman. I ever guard the character and persons of my students, especially females, with sleepless fatherly vigilance. For years I have advocated enacting a law to make every rapist a eunuch and then confine him to hard work in the Penitentiary for life. And the man who publishes that I have carelessly permitted this crime in my own house, deserves to be cow-hided out of Texas. The Lord himself did not prevent Eve from going astray with the Devil nor will any watchful care prevent some student from going astray, and some editors from lying. But our persecutors say because one frail Brazilian girl out of the vast army of students, has gone astray, "Baylor University is an unsafe place to educate young ladies," and that girls, of course, ought to be locked up in the Convent walls with the "holy"(?) environments of nuns and unmarried Fathers. In reply to this I can with inexpressible joy point to the noble army of queenly daughters I have educated in the last forty-four years, and say as the Mother of Gracchi did when challenged to show her jewels, pointing to her two sons saying: "These are my jewels." I can point to my noble army of 3,000 daughters scattered in almost every town and city of Texas and say: "These are my jewels." I can and do challenge any school in or out of Texas, Catholic or Protestant, to show purer brighter jewels than the daughters of Baylor University. These queenly daughters demonstrate that the man who says "Baylor University is an unsafe place to educate young ladies" is either a knave or a fool or both. Indeed such silly, stupid blunders as these, I have never seen. The leader in this crusade in portraying the horrors of Antonia's condition says "she is a fourteen year old child." In another place he says "she was thirteen years old when she came," and elsewhere he says "she has been here three years." What child in simple addition would make such a silly blunder. "13 plus 3 equals 14." Surely the "legs of the lame are not equal." Mrs. Daniel, returned Missionary, and an elegant lady who knew the Brazilian girl and the whole family in Brazil says she is eighteen years old, and the family is the filthiest and most depraved she ever knew. Again our persecutors and advocates of Catholic schools say "Judge Goodrich is a Baptist." I have known intimately and admired Judge Goodrich for thirty years, but I never heard before that he was a Baptist. But this of course was said merely to catch the gulls and deceive foreigners. Again I can point with joy to the fact that three-fourths of all our former students of Baylor University send us their daughters. Three of our noblest recent graduates are daughters of our former graduates. One of my earliest students says: "I want Dr. Burleson to educate all my daughters and all my grand-children." What higher evidence can there be that Baylor University is a suitable place to educate young ladies? But in conclusion I can but express my deep regret that while Baylor University has maintained such a record among our old students and has acquired a national reputation of high moral culture and training of her students, that our Waco papers should be found slandering and vilifying an institution that has done so much for the moral and material development of Waco. If this is tolerated by the good people of Waco, especially so soon after the reported failure of the Methodist College the good people of Texas will conclude that Waco is not the place for a great institution of learning. I sincerely hope therefore that all good students and citizens will rise up and vindicate Baylor University, and that those who have thoughtlessly or maliciously slandered her spotless character will repent and confess openly their sins and receive forgiveness, before they are everlastingly lost.

RUFUS C. BURLESON

Baylor University, Aug. 20, 1895

The Course of Justice

  The rebuttal, as is frequently the case, was far less effectual than the charge. Besides, it barely reached outside the town, and it was only through the *Iconoclast* that thousands of readers throughout the country could follow the reluctant and twisting course of law in one small pioneer town. For them the case became a symbol. It became a contest, as Brann told them, of "weakness vs. strength, of ignorance vs. knowledge, the good name of a fatherless girl vs. the reputation of a powerful denomination and a pretentious college." "Antonia Teixeira," he added, "cannot cast a single vote; the Baptist church holds the political destiny—and offices—of this judicial district in the hollow of its hand. Of course she may get justice, but it's a 100–1 shot."

Brann outlined the ramifications of the case faithfully:

August: ". . . the defendant has carried his case by habeas corpus before the district judge, and that official—a worthy Baptist brother—has rendered a Scotch verdict and ordered the release without bail of the alleged rapist. . . ."

October: ". . . The *Iconoclast* did not find fault with Baylor for the child's misfortune, fully realizing that accidents will occasionally occur even in the best regulated sectarian seminaries; but it did criticize Dr. Burleson for trying to shield that institution by branding as a wilful bawd the fatherless little foreigner committed to its care. It called attention to the fact that, instead of striving to bring to justice the lecherous scoundrel who dared invade the sacred precincts of Baylor and debauch a child, Dr. Burleson employed all his energy and influence to protect the man accused of the crime—to so prejudice the public mind that an impartial trial of the case would be impossible. . . ."

November: "The grand jury of this county recently returned a true bill against Steen Morris, charged with outraging Antonia Teixeira at Baylor University, and the case will probably be called for trial in a few days. . . . The *Iconoclast* is accused of being responsible for the defendant's indictment after he had been kangarooed out of court on habeas corpus. Be that as it may, it insists that he be given a patient hearing, and impartial trial. . . . Too many men have been sacrificed to popular clamor since the days of Christ. . . ."

January, 1896: "The case of the State vs. Steen Morris, charged with outraging a half-grown girl under the very nose of the good Dr. Burleson of Baylor, has been continued to the next term of court because one of the defendant's three attorneys had a pain in the umbilicus."

March: "The babe of Antonia Teixeira the duly ordained 'ward of the Baptist Church,' who was 'educated' in Dr. Burleson's kitchen 'for missionary work in Brazil' sleeps in a nameless grave. Having waited in vain for the Baptist Church to build it a monument, I have decided to take up the good work myself. It was no common babe, and deserves something better than pauper burial. It was begotten in a sacred institution, of a mother duly consecrated to the work of rescuing poor Catholics from the remorseless grip of Papacy. The Babe of the Alamo is celebrated in song and story; but no poet tunes the harp to sing the Babe of Baylor. It seems to me that the great Baptist seminary has been strangely derelict in its duty—has failed to properly advertise itself as a place where souls are made as well as saved. An institution that is striving successfully in a just cause should pause occasionally to throw bouquets at itself—to celebrate its triumphs. Baylor is far too modest. It received an ignorant little Catholic as raw material, and sent forth two Baptists as the finished product. That important triumph of mind over matter should be preserved in imperishable marble that will forever 'shine like a good deed in a naughty world.' To that end the *Iconoclast* herewith opens a subscription to build a monument to the dead babe's memory. I will contribute $50 if permitted to draw the design and write the inscription. I suggest a rectangular pyramid of pure white marble, surmounted by a life-size bust of Dr. Burleson, and bearing this inscription: 'Sacred to the memory of the infant daughter of

109

the 14-year-old ward of the Baptist Church, and an unknown member of the Baylor University Stud.'

"The monument should, of course, be located at the most conspicuous point in the grounds of that institution whose greatness and glory it is destined to commemorate. All subscriptions should be sent to Dr. Burleson, the monument, when completed, to be dedicated to his dutiful son-in-law, the Rev. S. L. Morris."

June: "H. Steen Morris, a young man who parts his name on the side, was tried in this city a few days ago on the charge of raping Antonia Teixeira. . . . Yes, Steen was to have 'easy rolling'; and when the jury dismissed him with a certificate of good moral character Dr. Burleson was going to sue the *Iconoclast* for damages—in the sum of 'steen million dollars, I s'pose. . . . To make assurance of 'easy rolling' doubly sure, those especially interested in securing the acquittal of the accused went to the friends and temporary guardians of the ruined girl and requested them to use their influence to secure a withdrawal of the charge that force was employed to accomplish her disgrace. . . . Rev. Zachariah C. Taylor and Dr. Rufus C. Burleson are two of the pious brethren who thus attempted to get Antonia to alter her testimony. When the case was submitted to the jury it developed that the defendant did not have such 'easy rolling' as the eminent divine had predicted. Seven of the jurors were not willing to turn him loose even to please the dominant political power, while the remaining five could not quite make up their minds that it was proper to put the brother of Dr. Burleson's pious son-in-law in the penitentiary. So the case goes over to the next term of court—while the

Baylorians redouble their efforts to get the plaintiff out of the country."

September: "An affidavit has been sworn by Antonia Teixeira before R. L. Allen, Esq., exonerating Mr. Steen Morris of the charge of assault to commit rape upon her person. . . .By some means it was secured. The Lord may have sent it in response to prayer. Possibly Antonia concluded that, before leaving Texas, she would give it to Capt. Blair as a keepsake. . . . When Capt. Blair asks the court to dismiss the case on the strength of this affidavit, let him be required to state why the drawer of the remarkable document purchased Antonia's ticket, and who furnished the funds. Of course, her long conference with Steen Morris and his attorney on the day before her departure may have been merely a social visit. If the currency question was discussed at all, it may have been from a purely theoretical standpoint. I have no desire to invade the sacred privacy that should behedge a lingering farewell of old friends. . . ."

Not everyone approved of Brann's hanging Baylor's dirty linen so high. In fact, not everyone approved of Brann's iconoclasm as such. Idol-smasher he might be, but a considerable segment of thinking people remained less than convinced that a continual tearing down had anything in common with building a better world. Ideals, they felt, were actually idols of the mind, idols that over the centuries had assumed a less graven look as they were transmuted to spiritual truths and aspirations. Thus the man who rampaged destructively among them, who was continually "against" and never "for," simply mocked the progress of thought.

One of the most vocal anti-Brann writers was James Armstrong, Jr., of San Antonio, who issued a pamphlet called *Brann X-Rayed*. Wrote Armstrong:

> Brann is a product of the times. Like all satirists and "iconoclasts," he is a literary maggot, produced and nourished by the fecund filth of social decay.
>
> . . . there is no difference . . . in giving a dime for an "Iconoclast" and "chipping in" to see a naked harlot dance the can-can; and the Apostle prostitutes his genius as much as she her body.
>
> . . . If a man had a mania for looking upon naked women, or was given to the commission of the crimes which have made the names of Onan and Lot jointly synonymous with infamy, Brann would correct him by photographing him in the act, and exhibiting the pictures in public places. A good scheme, no doubt, at so much a look; and with some enterprising genius to push it, the pictures would soon be circulating "throughout the United States and Canada." "Pictures for March Now In!! Hot Stuff!!!"

Later Armstrong turned to verse to prove his point:

> When Achilles was dipped in the river Styx
>   He was held by the heel.
> When Brann was dipped in the river Gall
>   he was held by the head.
> A reader may draw the moral with
>   a mustard plaster.

Pot Pourri

CHAPTER 8 Brann's more objective local critics accused him of slighting national targets in favor of the raw sensationalism of the Teixeira-Morris case. At the same time, anti-Baptists condemned him for giving too little space to the matter.

Actually, the *Iconoclast* devoted only a small portion of its columns to the affair. The rest was a titillating pot pourri of comment that ranged from Cleveland to kissing, from prohibition to prize-fighting.

For months the nation's press had kept the country minutely informed of the approaching birth of the President's child. Would it be another girl? A boy? What was the First Lady craving during her confinement? What would the child be named? The Hearst papers kept their most sentimental women reporters pouring out a cooing stream of fluttery nonsense, and after the event the press wires kept up almost hourly

113

bulletins. "Baby Cleveland awoke at 11:30 and wept softly," gurgled the telegraph. "The baby smiled intelligently and cooed to her happy father." It made Brann's gorge rise, and he discoursed upon the strange ways of the Associated Press.

We gather from the press dispatches that "at precisely 4:30 P.M. by the doctor's watch," on the seventh day of the seventh month of the year of grace 1895, a third baby girl was born to President and Mrs. Cleveland. Regardless of the Malthusian theory of population—and the existence of more girls in America than can reasonably hope to acquire dutiful husbands—we hasten to extend congratulations. It is possible that a male heir would have better pleased our "Liege, lord and sovereign born"; still, the man who holds three queens in the game of life—with the privilege of calling for cards—should feel encouraged. . . .

In the same issue he wrote "The Curse of Kissing," which began:

Every little while some smart Alec scientist mounts the bema to inform a foolish world that kissing is a dangerous pastime; that upon the roseate lips of beauty ever lurks the bacillus, flourishing skull and cross-bones—veritable flaming swords to keep poor Adam out of his Eden. According to these learned men the fairest maid is loaded to the muzzle with microbes, her kiss a Judas osculation, betraying the sighing swain who dares to browse. . . .

Brann's approach to matters of theology made the orthodox writhe. He lashed out at their contentment

114

with the letter of the Bible and their ignorance of its spirit.

The Chinese and the Kurds are doing today exactly what we are required to believe God commanded the Jews to do three and thirty centuries ago—cleaning out the unbelievers with sword and fire—an edict that has never been repealed. . . . "If there arise among you a prophet, or a dreamer of dreams . . . saying, Let us go after other gods which thou hast not known, and let us serve them. . . . that prophet or that dreamer of dreams shall be put to death. . . ." The religion of the Turks and the Chinese is just as dear to them as that of the Christian cult to its communicants; yet missionaries from Europe and America go among them uninvited and tell them that the time-honored faith of their fathers is but a tissue of falsehoods. . . . Is it any wonder—keeping Deuteronomy and the history of Medieval Christianity well in mind—that these self-expatriated apostles sometimes get it where the bottle got the cork?

When the whole country was consumed with interest over the approaching marriage of Consuelo Vanderbilt to the Duke of Marlborough, the *Iconoclast* gave its forty thousand readers something other than ecstatic conjectures on where the honeymoon would be spent. Lacking space for illustrations, Brann compensated by providing in words the lineage and physical attributes of the two principals:

The fiance of Miss Vanderbilt is descended . . . through a long line of titled cuckolds and shameless pimps, and now stands on the ragged edge of poverty,

115

bartering to parvenus for bread an empty dukedom bought with a female relative's dishonor. . . . In appearance he is a tough of the toughs. He has a head like a Bowery bouncer and the mug of an ape who has met with an accident.

And the Vanderbilts? Two hundred years ago an ignorant Hollander squatted on a patch of land at Flatbush, L.I., and engaged in the laudable enterprise of raising cabbages, while his better half added an occasional florin to the family hoard by peddling fish. . . . In the course of four generations the Van Der Bilts had accumulated sufficient boodle to buy a small ferryboat, and began at once to float on to fortune. The name was coupled up to save stationery in writing it. . . . She, Consuelo, is a long, gaunt, skinny young female whose face would frighten any animal but a pauper duke out for the "dough." Her muscular arms, snub nose, and big feet proclaim her plebeian origin, while if the countenance be a true index to the intellect, she is the mental equal of a half-baked Chinese idol.

The issue of November, 1896, was enlivened by the announcement of a beauty contest. "I will pay $500 for the blessed privilege of looking five minutes at the most beautiful woman in this world. Furthermore, I propose to ascertain her name and habitation, and make a pilgrimage to her shrine, no matter in what land or clime she lives."

Brann said he knew there existed "a creature more divinely fair than poet ever fabled or artist feigned," and he proposed to smoke her out. In hypnotic rhythm he added:

116

... I have heard her voice in the low sweet anthem of the summer sea at Night's high noon; I have caught fitful glimpses of her dark eyes' splendor in waking dreams, and when demons rode upon the storm of passion and murder shrieked within my soul, I have felt her dewy breath upon my fevered cheek, her cool tresses floating like leaves of the lotus-flower across my face. . . .

Ladies between the ages of seventeen and thirty-seven were invited to send in photos not more than one year old and to include address, height, weight, size of glove and shoe, and color of eyes and hair.

In the December issue the age limit was reduced to fifteen, "at the suggestion of several ladies who reside in foreign lands and under sunnier skies." Then Brann added:

Up to the present writing the countries represented in the contest are as follows: The United States, Canada, Mexico, Cuba, Venezuela, Peru, Brazil, Scotland, Ireland, Wales, France, Italy, and Denmark. . . . Of the cities, St. Louis furnishes the largest number of contestants, New Orleans second, Dallas and San Antonio being in a tie for third place. Thus far Waco hasn't a single aspirant for the Golden Apple.

As an afterthought:

Bust and waist measurements would materially assist the judges in determining the contest, but these may be given or withheld at the option of the aspirant. It is needless to say that all data furnished will be treated as confidential.

Side by side with this tongue-in-cheek contest the reader finds allusion after allusion that proves Brann's startling familiarity with literature. Recalling that his formal schooling stopped before he reached his teens, we find him referring casually to Molière's M. Jourdain, the brutalizing wand of Circe, Adam Smith, Tennyson, *Hamlet*, the Gordian knot, Sinbad, Draco, Boccaccio, du Maurier, *Henry VIII*, Bath-sheba, Luther, Lincoln, and Oedipus. He was acquainted with Hester Prynne, the demon Asmodeus, Lucrece, Sycorax, Pecksniff, Mrs. Grundy, Goethe, Ptolemy, Rabelais, and Ishtar. Yet one has no impression that Brann was a name-dropper attempting to overwhelm his readers with a battery of higher authorities. And surely copious reference to mythological or literary figures would not be reason for the skyrocketing circulation of the *Iconoclast*. These allusions were but flavoring; they were the herbs and spices of the "literary stew" he served piping hot every thirty days.

What made people read the Apostle so widely in 1897 was the same quality that makes him the delight of connoisseurs today: a magic, evocative ability with words and a style and literary approach that enabled him to combine those words into a whip of scorpions, a caress in the moonlight, or a mocking, Gargantuan, irresistible belly laugh. He was a ringmaster of phrases who could flick his pen and blend editorial force, an immense vocabulary, and a ribald streak into a monthly circus clowned by his enemies. The acts

changed as smoothly as the turning of the page, and
the band was wistful, militant, or raucous, depending
on the mood of the master.

There was enough Bach and Beethoven at the circus to draw the sophisticates; there was enough bump-
and-grind burlesque to ensure stamping in the gallery.
And what gave Brann's circus a fascinating Lewis Carroll touch was the frequent incongruous juxtaposition
of the two.

What cultivated man familiar with Epictetus, de
La Rochefoucauld, or Lao-tse could fail to appreciate
reflections such as these couched in the style unique to
Brann's *Iconoclast:*

PRIDE

Pride is the sheet-anchor of morality, the dynamics
of noble deeds. When love fails and hope flies, pride
still lingers, the savage rearguard of a human soul, and
dies in the last ditch.

CHRISTIAN SCIENCE

The opinion seems to be gaining ground that the
Christian Scientists should be incarcerated as lunatics
whose hallucination is dangerous to life. This idea
contravenes the plans of an all-wise Providence. They
are fool-killers employed by nature in the extermina-
tion of the unfit. They are the executives of the divine
law of evolution. Those who fall victims to this
Mumbo-Jumbo business fully deserve their fate. It is
urged that thousands of helpless children have been
slain by this pseudo-scientific superstition. Quite true;
but the children sacrificed to this modern Moloch were

begotten by Christian Scientists, are the offspring of weak intellects, and an evil tree cannot bring forth good fruit. We may sorrow for their sufferings, but are compelled to admit that the race is benefitted by their demise.

BYRON

If not altogether impractical and intellectually oblique could he have so heartily despised an eminently respectable society that was carefully preserving its game, clipping coupons and dressing quite up to date? Had there not been more than one screw loose in the man's head would he have squandered his fortune and lost his life trying to free Greece from the tyranny of the Turk? What was Hecuba to him, or he to Hecuba? Why should he prate of Burning Sappho when the old girl had been in the water for six-and-twenty centuries? . . . Perhaps of all Byron's poems Don Juan is most read—an apt illustration of the Shakespearean axiom that the evil men do lives after them. . . .

HERESY

An heretic, my dear sir, is a fellow who disagrees with you regarding something which neither of you knows anything about. The term, however, is usually applied to a member of a dissenting minority in matters religious.

WOMEN'S SUFFRAGE

Give a woman youth and beauty and she asks not —needs not—political power; but when, still a maid, her mirror tells her she could not pass for five-and-forty in the moonlight; when her bracelet slips over her elbows and a thumb-ring would make her a garter; when she becomes either a perambulating tub of un-

wholesome lard or has to pad her diaphragm to cast a
shadow, she is apt to be morbidly sensitive to

"The oppressor's wrong, the proud man's contumely,
The pangs of despised love, the law's delay."

SOCIETY REPORTING

Mrs. Crupper's beauty is of that voluptuous type
known to the euphuists as Junoesque, but called by the
vulgar herd Oleomargaramic. Her ample figure was
attired in a glove-fitting plum-colored bikeing suit of
Belfast corduroy, trimmed with sable fur, with belly-
band of untanned leather fastened with a massive
buckle made in an adjacent blacksmith shop. . . . A dia-
mond scarf-pin in the form of a crupper loomed up like
the headlight of a trolley car, while her left thumb
supported a massive ring of beaten gold as large as a
cuspidor. . . .

IMMORTALITY

I do not undervalue human life and effort and as-
piration. I do not mock the blind struggles of mortal
man to put on immortality . . . but I do insist that those
who assume the Almighty God made the solar system
for our sweet sakes should be tapped for the simples.
Surely the stupendous labors of the creator were under-
taken with grander object, a nobler aim than the
breeding on this comparatively unimportant planet of
a few harpers for Heaven and a host of hoodlums for
Hell. . . .

Down upon thy knees, aspiring pigmy, and give
thanks to God thou wast not born a beast—that the best
of terrestrial life is thine, with the joys of infancy, the
pride of manhood and the halo of age. Take the good
the gods provide and hold thy peace. If it be Heaven's

121

will that a happier world awaits thee beyond the tomb's pale portals, rejoice that thou art rewarded beyond thy deserts; if not, lie down like a tired child upon its mother's breast, and pass without a sigh into the eternal, the imperishable elements from which thou wert called—back into the great Life Ocean which is God.

THE DEMON RUM

. . . I have ever held to the opinion that a moderate use of stimulants is necessary to the physical well-being of the average man . . . not five percent of the world's intellectual titans were total abstainers. . . .

THE BLACK MAN

The black is here, and I see but one way to get rid of him, and that is to drive him *en masse* beyond the Ohio and give our nigger-loving neighbors an opportunity to test their fine theories by conditions. . . . But it is our duty, as honest men, to give her [the North] an idea what to expect of her black "images of God." She will have to build more prisons and poor-houses. She will have to chain Bunker Hill monument to the center of gravity or they'll steal it. She will have to put sheet-iron lingerie on her marble Goddess of Liberty or some morning she'll find the old girl with her head mashed in and bearing marks of sexual violence. . . .

DIVORCE

Wedlock is holy only where there exists mutual love and respect. Such unions do not need to be reinforced by strict marriage laws. . . . Those who protest so bitterly against divorce, who would compel people to live together after love has flown, appear to think the marriage ceremony a thaumaturgic incantation which sanctifies debauchery, a modern correlative of the ancient rites of Bacchus.

WACO, TEXAS

Waco, we would have you know, is the religious storm-centre of the Universe, and one of the few places that licenses prostitutes—a fact for the consideration of students of cause and effect. . . .

Of course Waco, like other places, has its drawbacks; but, taken by and large, there is no better. While it is true that you cannot secure a bath, shave or clean shirt here on Sunday, the saloons and churches are open, and the Reservation hath all seasons for its own. . . .

All trains stop at Waco. You will recognize the place by a structure that resembles a Kansas section-house that has been held by the vandal Time while criminally assaulted by a cyclone. . . .

Some day we'll bury the hypocritical mossbacks who have long played Old Man of the Sea to Waco's Sinbad—snivelling about their Jesue while cutting the throat of the town with a cold-blooded villainy that makes every man possessing a dollar afraid to pass through the place with the car windows open. . . .

"Sexual Purity and Gun-powder"

CHAPTER 9

Yet Waco, Texas, served perhaps better than any other place as a setting for the mind that was Brann's. It provided the goad of loneliness. At the same time it was a suitably restless town, moved by the spirit of optimism and growth and vitality that characterized Texas in the late 1800's.

It was a town that lived off cotton and cattle, a town with a red-light district that all but rubbed shoulders with the Opera House. Waco was—like many small frontier communities—dominated by a handful of wealthy families, parvenus-to-riches whose family legends involved ferry service, trading posts, and hand-to-hand combats with the Indians. The fact that Father or Grandfather had come to Texas from Missouri or Oklahoma or Mississippi searching for a bright new life frequently raised the unspoken question "Why?" but did nothing to tarnish the pride in the fact that

124

Father or Grandfather had done rather well once he established himself. It was a lineage of action rather than of antecedent. Second sons, adventurers, explorers, seekers—a Freudian could easily explain why they were so contemptuous of the gas-lit flabby folk up East whose blood was so blue, who didn't know a branding iron from a chuck wagon.

Brann himself realized that Waco was the best setting for his work.

I am a little afraid that the *Iconoclast* would lose its characteristic flavor if I moved it to one of the big Eastern cities. You will remember that the experiment was tried with the Arkansas *Traveller*, which was moved from Little Rock to Chicago, and promptly fell flat. The same thing happened to the Texas *Siftings*, when it was taken from Austin to New York. I am inclined to believe that a publication acquires a savor of the soil in which it springs, and it is a mighty risky business to try to transplant it.

From a financial point of view Waco had been kind to Brann. He is remembered walking to the bank, arms loaded with subscription dollars in the currency of a dozen lands. He said himself that for the first time in his life he had money and that he felt therefore a kind of obligation to Waco. As the *Iconoclast* spread throughout the land he moved his family from the boardinghouse on Austin Street to a large house of rich red brick and shaped roughly like a T with the stem facing North Fifth Street. Almost the whole end of the

125

stem was composed of two large bay windows, one above the other. The path leading from the iron gate divided at the window and each half curved around the stem of the house to the two-story porches that fronted the two arms of the T. There were chrysanthemums growing at the base of the window in front, and English ivy had been started up the bare brick. On one side of the house and a little in front was a pecan tree as high as the roof, and on the other side was a large oak whose branches almost reached the street.

The spring and summer of 1897 were the happiest Will Brann and his family had ever spent together. For the first time since they had left Rochelle, Illinois, he and Carrie were able to entertain their friends in a home of their own. Will could feel that at last he was giving Gracie and Billy an environment suitable to his hopes for them. The dream was coming true.

They bought furniture and they bought rugs and they bought draperies. They discussed color combinations, groupings, and styles with all the enthusiasm and chin-stroking that such matters have brought forth since the first woman decided to replace that old bison skin across the cave opening with a newer, more stylish hide. Carrie invented salads and created centerpieces with all the agony and delight that falls to the lot of brides, whether their home is waiting for them after the honeymoon or after a decade.

Bill Ward, Brann's business manager and constant companion, was invited to live with them in the new house, and he accepted. The big-boned two-hundred-pounder from Corsicana was more than a business associate. He was an uncle to the children, an adviser to Carrie, and a husky bodyguard for the Apostle whenever a particularly hot issue in the *Iconoclast* made protection necessary.

Of this period Ward later recalled a typical incident.

I remember in the early morning once he came into my room and silently beckoned me into his study. There in the vines at the window, scarce three feet from his desk, sat one of our Southern Orioles—a feathered songster, trilling forth the gladness of his heart in song. Brann watched the bird and drank in the music of his song. I saw his face light up with exquisite tenderness, and I knew that he accepted this matin song as a message from his Maker.

For Gracie, ten, and Billy, five, it was a summer of complete enchantment. The grounds became a fairyland. Before bedtime the family would gather with Will on the circular bench about the great cedar, and he would people the dusk with trolls and wee folk, animals that could talk more wisely than people, good spirits, and goblins. Sometimes they acted out the stories. Theseus, with the aid of Ariadne and a spool of thread, found his way through an aromatic labyrinth of gardenias and crape myrtle to slay the wicked minotaur. Oberon watched jealously as Titania commanded Pease-blossom, Mustard-seed, Cobweb, and Moth to do the bidding of the astonished Bottom. They learned Ariel's song, "Full fathom five thy father lies," and they listened entranced as Brann recited Prospero's moving speech, ". . . These our actors, as I foretold you, were all spirits and are melted into air, into thin air; and, like the baseless fabric of this vision, the cloud-capped towers, the gorgeous palaces, the solemn temples, the great globe itself. . . ."

For his editorial and mailing offices, Brann rented a suite in the Provident Building, a great U-shaped structure of rough gray stone at Fourth and Franklin streets. The *Iconoclast* was managed from rooms 29, 30, and 31 on the second floor inside of the west arm of the U. Brann and Ward could either walk the mile to the office or take the streetcar, which ran down Fifth to the center of town. Often Brann was driven in his hack by an old Negro named Willie, who was yardman and family factotum.

As the journal prospered, Brann enlarged his staff. A Mr. Milstead and a young man named John Guerin were employed, mainly to supervise distribution and mailing, which was becoming a tremendous task. At the office Brann wrote brief items for "Salmagundi" or "Editorial Etchings" and his correspondence, which was voluminous. The longer articles he wrote at home, either under the cedar or in the room that formed the upper part of the stem facing the street. His desk was close to the bay window, and between paragraphs he could rest his eyes on the leaves of the oak that brushed against the glass beside him.

As the *Iconoclast* became well known, Brann's absences from the new house on lecture engagements became frequent. He spoke at Fourth of July celebrations, at anti-prohibition rallies, at political gatherings, at Chautauquas, and before ladies' reading clubs.

The same cold-water shock that he achieved in his writing by tumbling slang and poetry together marked his public speaking. He was a handsome, tall man customarily dressed in black, and his voice was deep and resonant. He had thick brown hair and brown eyes that were said to be hypnotic, lighted by some inner fire. They were the gentle eyes of a father, the wild eyes of a zealot, the despairing, cynical eyes of a reformer smashing his spirit against the apathy of the world.

One of his earliest speeches was "Old Glory," delivered at San Antonio on July 4, 1893. In it he deplored avaricious politicians.

Theoretically we have the best government on the globe, but it is so brutally mismanaged by our blessed public servants that it produces the same evil conditions that have damned the worst. . . . We have achieved liberty, but have yet to learn in this strange new land the true significance of life. . . . But before God, I do believe that this selfish, this Mammon-serving age will pass . . . when Americans will be in spirit and in truth a band of brothers, the wrongs of one the concern of all; when brains and patriotism will take precedence of boodle and partisanship in our national politics; when labor will no longer fear the cormorant nor capital the commune. . . .

In a period of feverish political and economic recovery dating from the post-war years when Governor Davis ruled Texas by militia, it is noteworthy but not surprising that the *Iconoclast* devoted very little space to political issues. Except for his hobby-like preoccupation with America's fiscal policies, Brann's interest in political questions of the day was as dispassionate as that of a poet or a priest. Brann was a social satirist; he preferred to ridicule Mrs. Grundy rather than President Cleveland.

The Apostle dismissed the average politician as a man of little learning and less moral fiber. When he discussed Jeffersonian democracy, as he did in April, 1896, he told the reader that Jefferson was not an atheist, that he believed in freedom of the brain as well as of the hand. Instead of discussing with his readers Governor Culberson's record as a trust-buster, we find him commenting on the Governor's refusal to pardon a man who "had been sentenced to the pen by a jury of his peers for slaying the supposed seducer of his daughter." And the essay's title removed any reader's fear of plunging into political meditation: "Sexual Purity and Gunpowder."

Brann's readers wanted "Sexual Purity and Gunpowder," and not "An Inquiry into the Populist Attitude toward the Railroad Commission." The Apostle was delighted to oblige, either in print or from the rostrum.

An address that grew to be a favorite on his tours and was later included in his collection of *Speeches and Lectures* was "Humbugs and Humbuggery," a long verbal voyage down the social river with all guns firing. Here is a partial list of the topics mentioned in "Humbugs and Humbuggery," with a pertinent thought or two addressed to each.

MARRIAGE
Marriage is, perhaps, the only game of chance ever invented at which it is possible for both players to lose.

HEROES
Leonidas were lost to history but for the three hundred nameless braves who backed his bluff.

FRIENDSHIP
I am sometimes tempted to believe that the only friendship that will stand fire is that of a yellow dog for a pauper negro. Strike a friend for a small loan and his affection grows suddenly cold; lose your fortune and your sweetheart sends you word that she will be a sister to you. . . .

STREET-CORNER POLITICIANS
. . . the incarnation of fraud, the apotheosis of audacity, is the street-corner politician. He towers above his fellow fakes like Saul above his brethren. I have been time and again instructed in the most intricate problems of public polity—questions that have perplexed the wisest statesmen of the world—by men who have never read a single standard work on political econ-

omy, and who could not tell to save their souls—granting that they possess such perishable property—whether Adam Smith wrote the "Wealth of Nations" or the Lord's Prayer.

DOCTORS

Once after holding forth at some length on Humbugs a physician said to me:

"Ah-er—you-ah—didn't mention the medical profession."

"No," I replied, "the power of language hath its limits." . . . I much doubt whether one-half the M.D.'s now sending people to the drug store with their cipher dispatches, could tell what was the matter with a suffering mortal were he transparent as glass and lit up by electricity.

EDUCATION

If it be a waste of lather to shave an ass, what must it be to educate an idiot? . . . We pore over books too much and reflect too little; depend too much on others, too little upon ourselves. . . . Neither the public nor any other school system has produced one really great man. Those who occupy the dais-throne among the immortals contended single-handed with the darkness of ignorance and the devil of dogmatism.

ATHEISM

About the time a youngster first feels an irresistible impulse to make a fool of himself whenever a female smiles upon him . . . he attempts to rip religion up by the roots and reform the world while you wait. . . . Most youths have to pass through a period of doubt and denial—catch the infidel humor just as they do the measles and mumps; but they eventually learn that the fear of God is the beginning of wisdom.

. . . An atheist once solemnly assured me that he couldn't possibly *believe* anything which he couldn't *prove;* but when I asked him what led him to take such a lively interest in the welfare of his wife's children, he became almost as angry as a Calvinist whose confession of faith had been called in question.

THE DEVIL

I confess to a sneaking respect for Satan, for he is pre-eminently a success in his chosen profession. . . . He sat into the game with a cash capital of one snake; now he's got half the globe grabbed and an option on the other half. . . . I have been called a defender of the devil; but I hope that won't prejudice the ladies against me, as it was a woman that discovered him.

LOVE

Like sea-sickness, everybody laughs at it but those who have got it. When Cupid lets slip a sure-enough shaft it goes thro' a fellow's heart like a Kansas cyclone thro' a colored camp-meeting, and all the powers of Hades can never head it off. Love is the most sacred word ever framed by celestial lips. It's the law of life, the harmony of heaven, the breath of which the universe was born, the divine essence increate of the ever-living God. . . . But love is like all other sweet things—unless you get the very best brand it sours awful easy.

PIETY

Too many people presume that they are full of the grace of God when they're only bilious. . . . They put up long prayers on Sunday; that's piety. They bamboozle a green gosling out of his birthright on Monday; that's business. . . . They even acquire two voices—a brisk business accent and a Sunday whine that would make a cub wolf climb a tree.

HARSHNESS

People frequently say to me, "Brann, your attacks are too harsh. You should use more persuasion and less pizen." Perhaps so; but I have not yet mastered the esoteric of choking a bad dog to death with good butter. Persuasion is well enough if you're a'courting—or in the hands of the vigilantes; but turning it loose on the average fraud were too much like a tenderfoot trying to move a string of freight steers with moral suasion. He takes up his whip, gently snaps it as tho' he feared it were loaded, and talks to his cattle like a Boston phi-lanthropist to a poor relation. The steers look round at him, wonder, in a vague way, if he's worth eating, and stand at ease. An old freighter who's been over the "divide" and got his profanity down to a fine art, grabs that goad, cracks it like a rifled cannon reaching for a raw recruit and spills a string of cuss words calculated to precipitate the final conflagration. You expect to see him struck dead—but those steers don't. They're firmly persuaded that he's going to outlive 'em if they don't get down and paw gravel and they get a Nancy Hanks hustle on 'em. Never attempt to move an ox-team with moral suasion, or to drown the cohorts of the devil in the milk of human kindness. It won't work.

Another of Brann's well-known lectures was "Speaking of Gall," a survey of "sublimated audacity, transcendent impudence, immaculate nerve, and triple-plated cheek" as revealed in politics, poetry, Anglophilia, religion, social customs and morals, the law, the newspaper profession, and prize-fighting. Its tenor was similar to "Humbugs and Humbuggery," in that it was a sometimes humorous, sometimes earnest denunciation of sham and hypocrisy.

Because his was a unique voice crying out like a nineteenth-century Jeremiah, but blessed with a wry sense of humor that made his scorn palatable, the public swarmed to his lectures. It is probable that they considered him more performer than prophet, and what more entertaining way to spend an evening than to hear the heralded Apostle ring out for an hour and a half with invective and anecdote?

His fee became a hundred dollars per appearance, and during the latter half of 1897 Ward's managership kept him on tour about half of every month.

Another substantial source of income that grew with the success of the *Iconoclast* was the sale of pamphlets such as *Brann's Speeches and Lectures*, twenty-five cents; *Brann's Annual—An Infallible Ennui Antidote—Double Distilled Chain Lightning*, twenty-five cents; and *Potiphar's Wife—Brann's Breeziest Pamphlet*, at newsdealers', five cents, by mail, six cents.

Potiphar's Wife—The Story of Joseph Revised was a six-thousand-word how-it-might-really-have-happened account of the difficulty between Joseph and "Mrs. Potiphar." It was undoubtedly written to make money, and for no other reason. Brann's story is a sensuous, titillating literary aphrodisiac composed of sentences that warm the reader's blood with their pulsing rhythm as they pound to the story's climax.

The young wife and the young slave have been drawn closer and closer together until one day

. . . she bends low and whispers the line upon his lips, while her fragrant breath, beating upon his cheek, sinks into his blood like the jasmine's perfume. . . . What wonder that the callow shepherd lad, unskilled in woman's wile, believed that his mistress loved him? . . . Her lips are not a thread of scarlet, chaste as childhood, and dewy as the dawn, but the deep sullen red of a city swept with flames. Her breasts are not like young roes that feed among the lilies, but ivory hemispheres threaded with purple fire and tinged with sunset's tawny gold. Reverently as though touching divinity's robe, Joseph caresses the wanton curls that stream like an inky storm-cloud over the shapely shoulders. . . .

. . . The room swims before her eyes and fills with mocking demons that welcome her to the realm of darkness . . . while beneath the accursed magic of the kisses that burn upon her lips, her blood becomes boiling wine and rushes hissing through a heart of ice.

With an involuntary cry of rage and shame . . . she flings herself sobbing and moaning upon the marble floor. The drowsy slave starts up as from a dream, quivering in every limb like a coward looking upon his death. He tries to raise the groveling victim of his unbridled lust, but she beats him back. . . . The culprit glances with haggard face and wildly pleading eyes at the woman, once so imperial in her pride, now cowering, a thing acursed, clothed only with her shame and flood of ebon hair. The great sun, that hung in mid-heaven like a disc of burnished brass when she first forgot her duty, descends like a monstrous wheel of blood upon the western desert and through the casement pours a ruddy glow over the prostrate figure—a marble Venus blushing rosy red.

But when Potiphar comes upon the scene, she has already repented of the scene.

She lays her hand lightly upon his arm, great Egypt's shield, a pillar of living brass; she nestles in the grizzly beard like some bright flower in a weird forest; she kisses the bronzed cheek as Judas did that of our dear Lord and soothes him with pretty truths that are wholly lies.

Joseph is a good boy, but sometimes overbold, poor child! Perhaps her beauty charmed away his senses and made him forget his duty. Let it pass; for, by the mystic mark of Apis, she frightened the boy out of his foolish fever.

. . . Potiphar determines to watch his wife . . . he has learned from her own confession that she is a flirt, and he knows full well that a married coquette is half courtesan. Suspecting that Joseph's offense is graver than his wife set forth, he casts him into prison. The inexperienced youth, believing the full extent of his guilt has been blazoned to the world, and frightened beyond his wits by armed men and clank of chains, protests with tears and sighs that he is more sinned against than sinning. It is the old story of Adam improved upon—he not only damns the woman, but denies the apple. . . .

137

At only a nickel a copy (or six cents by mail), we can be certain that Brann's breezy story-of-many-colors was not a financial tragedy.

The Abduction

 From time to time during the summer of 1897 the *Iconoclast* carried articles that anguished the Baptists. Brann violently attacked a plan, set forth in Cranfill's *Baptist Standard*, that Waco citizens of that faith buy only from merchants of like denomination. He ridiculed Waco's Sunday blue laws. He mocked their preoccupation with the sale of liquor while they winked at the Reservation and at the slums that fringed the city. He reminded them bitterly of Antonia Teixeira, whose "diploma" was a three-pound child.

In consequence he found letters on his desk, such as this one from Nacogdoches, Texas: "The Baptists of this town have forced your agent to promise to discontinue selling the *Iconoclast* under penalty of expulsion from the church." His reply was prompt: ". . . contumacious recalcitrants are invariably boycotted in

139

business by the hydrocephalous sect which boasts that it was the first to establish liberty of conscience and freedom of speech in this country, yet which has been striving desperately for a hundred years to banish the last vestige of individuality and transform this nation into a pharisaical theocracy with some prurient hypocrite as its hierarch. . . ."

The opening of classes at Baylor in September, 1897, was coincident with a struggle over the presidency. Dr. Rufus Burleson, tired and seventy-four, wished to retire from his labors, and Dr. B. H. Carroll, chairman of the board of trustees, wanted to succeed to the presidency.

In the October *Iconoclast* Brann chose to commemorate both the argument and the peak enrollment:

I note with unfeigned pleasure that, according to claims of Baylor University, it opens the present season with a larger contingent of students, male and female, than ever before. This proves that Texas Baptists are determined to support it at any sacrifice—that they believe it better that their daughters should be exposed to its historic dangers and their sons condemned to grow up in ignorance than that this manufactory of ministers and Magdalenes should be permitted to perish. . . .

The *Iconoclast* would like to see Baylor University, so called, become an honor to Texas instead of an educational eye-sore, would like to hear it spoken of with reverence instead of sneeringly referred to by men

140

about town as worse than a harem. Probably Baylor has never been so bad as many imagined, that the joint-keepers in the Reservation have been mistaken in regarding it as a rival, that the number of female students sent away to conceal their shame has been exaggerated; still I imagine that both its morale and its educational advantages are susceptible of considerable improvement. . . .

Unfortunately there is more brazen quackery in our sectarian colleges than was ever dreamed of by Cagliostro. The faculty of such institutions is usually composed of superficially educated people who know even less than is contained in the text-books. As a rule they are employed because they will serve at a beggarly price, but sometimes because their employers are themselves too ignorant to properly pass upon the qualifications of others. You cannot estimate a man's intellect by the length of his purse, by the amount of money he has made and saved; but it is quite safe to judge a man's skill in his vocation by the salary he can command. . . .

There is no reason, however, why the institution should be in the future so intellectually and morally unprofitable as in the past. Change is the order of the universe, and as Baylor cannot very well become worse it must of necessity become better. It will have the unswerving support of the *Iconoclast* in every effort to place itself upon a higher educational plane, to honestly earn the money it pockets as tuition fees. I am even willing to conduct a night school free of charge during three months in the year for the instruction of its faculty if each member thereof will give bond not to seek a better paying situation elsewhere as soon as he learns something. . . .

I greatly regret that my Baptist brethren, Drs. Hayden and Cranfill, Burleson and Carroll, should have gotten into a spiteful and un-christian snarl over so pitiful a thing as Baylor's $2,000 presidency—that they should give to the world such a flagrant imitation of a lot of cut throat unregenerates out for the long green. . . .

If you must fight and scratch like a brace of Kilkenny cats, why the hell don't you sneak quietly into the woods and fight it out instead of exhibiting your blatant jackasserie to the simple people of Dallas and McLennan counties and thereby bringing our blessed church into contempt! Gadzooks! If you splenetic-hearted old duffers don't sand your hands and take a fresh grip on your Christian charity I'll resign my position as chief priest of the Baptist church and become a Mormon elder. I'll just be coffer-damned if I propose to remain at the head of a church whose educators, preachers, and editors are forever hacking away at each other's goozle with a hand-ax and slinging slime like a lot of colored courtesans. . . .

On Friday, October 1, the *Iconoclast* containing these reflections reached the streets of Waco. For the average Waco reader Brann need not have troubled to write the articles on George Gould, the new Cleveland baby, Walter S. Halliwell (the Ward McAllister of Kansas City), the single tax, or, for that matter, anything other than the comparatively brief comments on Baylor University. They stood out as though printed in red. The fact that the *Iconoclast* was read throughout America, as well as in many foreign countries, compounded the rage of the Baptists. Waco itself was being held up to the laughter and scorn of all tolerant, thinking people.

Brann stayed at home the next morning. It was his custom to do so on Saturdays if possible, since Billy and Gracie had no school that day and it gave him an opportunity to be with them. It was a beautiful autumn morning, heavy with mist at first, and then sunny and warm. He always felt especially relaxed and carefree the day after an issue had gone to press. The weight was lifted from his shoulders; it was up to Ward and Milstead and Guerin from now on.

But early in the afternoon he decided to visit his office and also to drop by his printers', Knight and Womack, to discuss some business details.

Just inside the door of Knight and Womack's rested a battered leather sofa, and the three men were sitting upon it when the street door banged open and two husky young men approached Brann.

One of them covered him with a pistol while the other pulled him to his feet and to the door. They pushed him outside, then south on the sidewalk about thirty feet to a waiting hack. The boys placed Brann between them on the back seat, the larger still holding Brann's arm while the other kept the pistol aimed at his stomach. The driver cracked the whip and the carriage jerked forward. They drove rapidly west along the Katy tracks for one block and then turned south down Fifth Street. The carriage began to careen wildly as the frightened horse broke into full gallop under the lash. The transition from the quiet discussion on the sofa to the swaying carriage had taken less than sixty seconds.

Brann's first reaction was one of anger at having let them catch him so completely unaware. Yet ever since the first difficulty with the Baptists and with Baylor he had been expecting trouble in some form. He had been warned often enough. Gerald and Shaw had warned him. Ward had warned him. Almost daily there had been some kind of anonymous threat in his mail. But he had never in the world expected to be kidnaped by a trio of excited schoolboys and taken on a frenzied ride down a public street. Certainly Womack and Knight would sound the alarm, and he had plenty of friends who would come to his rescue. Still, it would make him a laughingstock for months if they got away with their adolescent prank.

They were approaching the campus in front of Main and Georgia Burleson Hall, and he saw knots of students milling about on the green lawn. As the carriage drew to a stop they surrounded it.

He felt himself pushed to the sidewalk, and the excited mob crushed about him. A rope was thrown about his body and drawn so tight that his elbows dug into his sides. They wound it around him and then tied it so that he could be drawn about by the long free end.

Laughing and shouting, a dozen boys grabbed the rope and drew him toward the steps of Main.

"It's too low. The rope's too low!" "Yeah, put it around his neck!" "Lynch the atheist!" "Hang him!" A hundred voices took up the cry. They chanted in unison: "Hang him! Hang him! Hang him! Hang him!"

From the corner of Fifth and Speight it looked simply as though the students were having another of their class battles or perhaps one of those initiations that the young men delighted in so much. The west sun cast the shadow of Main almost halfway to Fifth Street. The tops of the elm and hackberry trees were still shimmering with light, and as they pulled and hauled they moved in and out of the patches of light in a savage kind of mass dance.

At first only the nearest and bravest touched Brann. Then, daring each other, urging each other, gaining confidence from each other, more and more reached out and cuffed him with their hands or struck him with their canes. He felt a cut open on his forehead, then another on his lip. When he bent his head to avoid taking the blows in the face they raised welts on his neck. The boys pulling the rope jerked it, trying to throw him off balance. Brann staggered. He saw the intent expressions on their faces, the fascinated look of those who inflict pain. They were breathing heavily, and their voices became shrill.

In the whirlpool of sticks and elbows and animal

cries he struggled, more from instinct than reason. In another few moments the courage of the mob would reach its bestial peak.

He was aware that lynchings were not new to these youths. At least twice a week the newspapers carried accounts of a lynching somewhere. The gruesome variations of technique were given in detail, and the general tone deplored the necessity rather than the occurrence.

There was a moment of confusion when they reached the steps. "Where in hell are the tar and feathers?" someone shouted.

A boy shook his head. "We had them hidden under the bridge over there but somebody moved them. The boys are still looking."

The first boy swore. "Wait a minute," he shouted to the mob. "Listen, everybody."

The crowd gathered about the steps in a semicircle, Brann in the center.

"Listen," shouted the leader. "We were going to tar and feather this Yankee and pack him out of town on a rail. Now somebody's gone and stolen the tar." Howls of disappointment went up. "So I guess we'll just have to give him his walking papers without any of the trimmings."

"Hang him! Hang him!" Several of the boys took the rope again and began tugging Brann down the steps toward a tall tree. The grinning faces were turned upward, looking for a suitable limb. "There's one!" said

146

some. "Here, this one!" cried others, and for a moment each pulled in a different direction. Several of them had pushed a bench beneath a hackberry limb. They drew him toward it.

"Boys! Boys! Listen to me!" Brann heard a more authoritative voice than any of the others. "It's Professor Brooks," said a boy near Brann. Those with the rope hesitated and turned to look. On the steps stood a man with his arms outstretched. "We don't want a hanging, boys! Let's be fair about this. We don't want a hanging. Professor Tanner and I won't stand by and see you lynch a man, whatever he's done, as long as there are proper courts of law in this county." His eye and voice held them. At the same moment Brann saw that Professor Tanner, a short, bearded man, had stationed himself by the bench. Frustrated, they drew Brann back toward the steps of Main.

"A firing squad!" someone cried. "Stand him up against a wall and shoot him!"

But Brann saw the contingent that rushed toward the armory turned back. Another teacher blocked the entrance. Arms spreadeagled across the opening, he stood firm. "Sorry, boys," he said calmly. "No bloodshed."

"How did Pool hear about this?" said a voice in dismay.

"Make him swear to leave town!" a boy shouted. "Make him eat his words and swear to clear out of town!"

"Tell him to sign this," another cried. "A lie bill!" A hand passed up a sheet of paper, and one of the leaders glanced at it. "All right." He held the paper in front of Brann's bleeding face. "Here! Sign this, and we may let you get out of town in one piece."

"Untie his arms!" "Make him write it in blood!" They untied the rope. Someone pushed a pencil into his hand. "Sign it! It says you're a damned liar and that you'll leave town before sunset."

Brann passed his hand dazedly over his forehead. It came away sticky and red. "But this is—"

"Sign it!" Someone struck him in the back with a stone, or maybe it was a fist. He was beyond distinguishing. He took the pencil and scrawled "Brann" on the paper. "That's more like it," a voice said. "Now get going and never come back. You've got till sundown!"

Stumbling and half-blinded, he felt himself pushed toward the carriage. He got in. But before he could pick up the reins they slashed the horse, and the animal leaped away. Brann grasped the seat with both hands to avoid being thrown out. A great vicious roar of laughter rang in his ears as he was swept away, half-fainting, and swaying like a rag dummy someone had tied in jest to the plunging hack.

The Whipping

CHAPTER II  Brann's kidnaping was not a spontaneous affair.

A committee of six boys had been appointed to deal with the Apostle by the memberships of the two largest societies at Baylor—the Philomathesians and the Erisophesians. This committee appointed a subcommittee of three to effect the actual kidnaping.

It is not difficult to recreate the feelings of these young students against a man who branded their university a "manufactory of ministers and Magdalenes" because one Brazilian girl had accused a man—not even a student—of seducing her. There was no way they could humble him in the public prints, so they chose the only alternative—direct, physical action.

That Brann had friends even among the Baylorites is evidenced by the fact that the tar and feathers, hidden under a bridge for the occasion, were spirited away by his partisans. But they were surely an infinitesimal minority, who had formed allegiance that was the nearest outlet for high-spirited youthful liberalism.

That Brann's attacks on Baylor were—in spite of optimistic statistics on enrollment—actually creating a desperate situation was shown at an informal meeting of Waco's leading businessmen at the First Baptist Church on the Monday night following the kidnaping. They were invited by the trustees of Baylor, and the Honorable W. H. Jenkins, vice-president of the board, opened the meeting by explaining that "if such slanderings as appeared in the *Iconoclast* are to go unchallenged; if they are to receive no condemnation at the hands of the citizens of Waco, then your silence will be construed into approval and the trustees and faculty will find it difficult if not impossible to get students to enter the halls of Baylor even if they should have the disposition to do so."

Judge Marshall Surratt was elected to serve as chairman of the meeting, and he suggested temperance, even though "one of our citizens in his way, is attempting to tear down this institution."

Banker W. D. Lacy endorsed the opening remarks of Judge Jenkins. He was followed by J. E. Boynton, who commented that "virtue has been betrayed and sold for money."

The meeting was attended by several of the Baylor ringleaders, and one of the young men was called upon. "We may have done wrong," he said. "You may call us boys and beardless youths, but I want to say that I do not believe that any 200 men in Waco or elsewhere could have borne what we have from this man, and then have him in your possession like we did on last Saturday and let him get off as easily as we did. . . . We did not desire to kill him nor even hurt him, but we did propose to make him swallow his falsehoods."

The meeting concluded with the signing by those present of a testimonial: ". . . We are familiar with existing conditions, and we denounce the publication in question as grossly slanderous and deserving the condemnation of honest men and pure women."

On Tuesday, October 5, Brann ran a "card" in the *Waco Daily Telephone* clarifying his position:

It was not the students, but the management that I criticized. . . . In my opinion, such an institution should be so conducted that a case like that of Miss Teixeira could not possibly occur. . . . I am well aware that some of the noblest men and women of Texas have been students of Baylor; but in my opinion their nobility is not due to Baylor but to themselves. . . . I would deserve to be shot if I defamed the humblest girl within its walls.

But the "card" was poor poultice for the pride of the hotter heads, and one of the least soothed was young George Scarborough.

One version of the following incident has it that George was determined to hunt the editor down with a pistol and have it out with him because Brann had referred to the Baylor boys as "undiapered babes." His father, the Judge, promised that if George would forget gunplay, he personally would deliver a horsewhipping to the Apostle.

Whatever the immediate background, on Wednesday, October 6, the Judge and young George met Brann in the hall of their office building. The youngster drew a gun; the father raised his heavy cane. In a moment they had driven Brann down the stairway and out to Franklin Street, the father raining blows upon the Apostle.

John Scarborough was only fifty years old and he was wiry and strong. The cane stung like fifty scorpions as it fell. It burned the recent wounds like a hot iron and created fresh ones of its own. Brann staggered to the street, and the people there stopped in astonishment at the sight. Even if anyone had wanted to stop the attack, the sight of young George's pistol would have prevented it.

At that moment a hack drove up. Hardly pausing, the boy who drove it leaped from his seat, grasped the whip, and ran toward the three of them. "So you wouldn't leave town, eh?" he yelled, and the long leather snaked a brutal ring of fire around Brann's shoulders. Brann recognized him as one of the ringleaders of the Baylor attack.

Brann's horse and hack were tied a little way down Franklin. It was either stand and be beaten until he fell or dash for it and take the risk of being shot in the back. In the struggle Brann caught one end of the whip and swung it so that the boy jostled the Judge, and in the same instant Brann let go and dashed for his carriage.

When he tried to pull himself up to the seat, he felt an agonizing streak of pain shoot up his right arm. He looked down. His wrist hung at a sickening angle in his sleeve. With his left hand he picked up the reins, and then he stood and faced his tormentors.

"Truth will rise again!" he shouted. "Truth crushed to earth will rise again!" The effort left him exhausted. He jerked the reins weakly and the horse began to move; the jolting made the pain in his arm almost unbearable. With his left hand he laid it across his lap. Fighting off unconsciousness he drove out Fifth Street toward his home.

"Ropes, Revolvers, and Religion"

CHAPTER 12

There follow excerpts from Brann's published account of the affair entitled "Ropes, Revolvers, and Religion" in the November, 1897, *Iconoclast*.

I have just been enjoying the first holiday I have had in fifteen years. Owing to circumstances entirely beyond my control, I devoted the major part of the past month to digesting a couple of installments of Saving Grace presented by my Baptist brethren, and carefully rubbed in with revolvers and ropes, loaded canes and miscellaneous cudgels—with almost any old thing calculated to make a sinner reflect upon the status of his soul. . . .

My Baptist brethren desired to send me as a missionary to foreign lands, and their invitation was so urgent, their expressions of regard so fervent that I am now wearing my head in a sling and trying to write with my left hand. Although they declared that I had an imperative "call" to go, and would tempt Providence by loitering longer than one short day, I concluded to remain in Waco and preach them a few more of my popular sermons from that favorite text, "If ye forgive not men their trespasses, neither will your Father forgive your trespasses." . . .

The same old God-forsaken gang of moral perverts and intellectual misfits who more than two years ago brought a Canadian courtesan and an unfrocked priest to Waco to lecture on A.P.A. ism, and who threatened at one of these buzzard feasts to mob me for calling the latter a cowardly liar, were responsible for my being dragged with a rope by several hundred hoodlums up and down a Baptist college campus in this city Oct. 2, and for the brutal assault upon me five days later by a pack of would-be assassins who had waited until my back was unsuspectingly turned before they had the nerve to get out their guns. I can overlook the assault made by the college students, although most of them were grown men, because they were encouraged thereto by their elders. I have positively refused to prosecute them; but the last assault was led by a shyster lawyer of middle-age, a so-called "judge," a member of the board of managers of Baylor. I am seeking no trouble with any of them—they are perfectly safe in so far as I am concerned; still if the latter gang are not satisfied with their cowardly crime, if they regret that they were beaten off ere they quite succeeded in sending me to Kingdom Come, they have only to notify me where and when they can be found alone, and I'll give the whole accursed mob a show for their money. I'm too slight for a slugger—cannot lick a herd of steers with one pair o' hands; but I can make a shotgun sing Come to Christ. I am credibly informed that "at least half a dozen" of my meek and lowly Baptist brethren are but awaiting an opportunity to assassinate me, and that if successful they will plead in extenuation that I "have slandered Southern women." I walk the streets of Waco day by day, and I walk them alone. Let these cur-ristians shoot me in the back if they dare, then plead that damning lie as excuse for their craven cowardice. If the decent of this community fail to chase them to their holes and feed their viscera to the dogs, then I'd rather be dead and in hades forever than alive in Waco a single day. . . .

After the first outbreak the Baylor bullies of the lost manhood stripe and their milk-sick apologists held a windy powwow in a Baptist church, and there bipedal brutes with beards, creatures who have thus far succeeded in dodging the insane asylum, whom an inscrutable Providence has kept out of the penitentiary to ornament the amen-corner—many of whom do not pretend to pay their bills—some of whom owe me for the very meat upon the bones of their scorbutic brats—branded me as a falsifier while solemnly protesting that they had never read a line of my paper. . . .

These intellectual eunuchs, who couldn't father an idea if cast bodily into the womb of the goddess of wisdom, declared positively that I would be permitted to print nothing more about their beloved Baylor—and that without knowing whether I had advertised it over two continents as an oasis in a moral Sahara or a snake-hole in the Dismal Swamp. It was a beautiful, a refreshing sight. . . .

Were I not persona non grata I would like to witness the classroom performances of these young professors—chosen with owlish gravity by men who cannot write deer sur without the expenditure of enough nervo-muscular energy to raise a cotton crop, chewing off the tips of their tongues and blotting the paper with their proboscides. Yet for offering to open a night school for the benefit of the Baylorian faculty I was mobbed; for intimating that the board of managers had not socked with old Socrates and ripped with old Euripides I was assaulted by one of their number and his brave body guard and beaten with six-shooters and bludgeons. . . .

I would not destroy Baylor; I would make it better. I would deprive the ignorant and vicious of control. I would expel all the hoodlums whose brutality and cowardice have disgraced it. I would place at its head a thorough educator and strict disciplinarian, a man of broad views and who sets a good example by paying his bills. I would make its diplomas badges of honor as in the old days, instead of certificates of illiteracy at which public school children laugh. . . .

A word to the lady students of Baylor: Young ladies, this controversy does not in the least concern you. The *Iconoclast* has never questioned your good character. You are young, however, and mischievous people have led some of you to believe that it has done so. If you so believe, I am as much in duty bound to apologize as though I had really and intentionally wronged you. A gentleman should ever hasten to apologize to ladies who feel aggrieved; hence I sincerely crave your pardon for having printed the article which gave you offense. Upon learning that you read into it a meaning which I did not intend, I stopped the presses and curtailed the circulation of the October number as much as possible, proving my sincerity by a pecuniary sacrifice. I would not for the wealth of this world either do you a wilful injustice, or have you believe me capable of such a crime. May you prosper in your studies, graduate with honor, and bestow your hands upon men worthy of noble women. . . .

Let it go at that. They have had their say, I've had mine, and right here I drop the subject until another attempt is made to run me out of town. I make this concession, not that Baylor deserves it, but at the earnest request of the law-abiding element of this city.

"Six-Shooter Depot"

CHAPTER 13

 Whereas Brann was willing to "let it go at that," there were others who felt the matter was far from settled, and the most vocal and stubborn among them was "Big Sandy" Gerald—Judge Gerald—the lean, honest, free-thinking, terrible-tempered old soldier.

Gerald put his views in a hotly worded letter, which he had delivered to J. W. Harris, editor of the *Waco Times-Herald*. Harris had come to Waco with his brother, W. A. Harris, as general manager of the United States Life Insurance Company, with offices in rooms 69, 70, and 71 of the Provident Building. W. A. Harris was with the Southwest Department of the Home Life Insurance Company, and lived close to the Geralds at 203 Mitchell Avenue, in northwest Waco.

The Harrises moved in the best Waco circles. J. W. was "a big, fine-looking man with a flowing brown mustache and curly hair. He was bright and pushing and a ready speaker. He was a director of the Cotton Palace in 1895 and 1896 and kept himself in the limelight."

Harris assured the Judge that his letter would of course be published. But day after day passed and it did not appear, and so the Judge, perhaps after reconsidering what he had written, went to the newspaper and asked for the letter's return. Embarrassingly, J. W. did not have the communication. "It was in the hands of some of the important advertisers who were backing the paper for their criticism and approval which it had apparently not received, nor had it been returned to the newspaper office."

What followed was described by Judge Gerald in a handbill, which he had published and posted throughout the neighborhood.

TO THE PUBLIC
Waco, Texas, October 21, 1897

In relation to the difficulty which occurred between myself and the editor of the *Times-Herald*, about a communication left at his office, which he refused to publish and refused to return to me, I have this to say: That it is the universal rule among all editors to return rejected communications, if they are demanded, the writer either furnishing the stamps to carry them through the mails or upon making a personal demand for same; I will also assert, that no honorable editor will ever allow the communication that he rejects to willingly pass into the hands of another. When I left the communication at the *Times* office on Saturday night, I stated emphatically to Doctor Weathered, one of the business partners of the concern, that if it was not published, I wanted it returned to me, and this information was conveyed to the editor. On Monday morning I called for it, and was informed that I could not get it, that it was locked up in the desk of the editor, who was absent. I left a message that I wanted it, and held him responsible for its return to me. It was my property, and I had an unquestioned right to demand it, and I was determined to have it for reasons that were good to me, and which many persons who have since read that communication will know. I was refused time and again. Provoked beyond endurance, I at last told him—knowing that I was physically unable to engage in a fisticuff with him, to get his pistol, come out into the street, and we would make it a matter of life or death. He refused to do it. I then left, he followed me up, through the hallway to the stairway, still continuing to talk over the matter, still refusing to give me what was unquestionably mine, and at last waited until he got me in a position, where, even if my physical strength had been equal to his, he would have had a great advantage over me, he, by his own acts and his own conduct provoked me into saying words that he of course justified himself in striking me. When he delivered the first blow—and I believe he had some foreign substance in his hand—I felt my eye closed from the blood rushing from the gash above my eyebrow; having practically but one hand, then being deprived of one eye, and being nearly double his age, and about one-fourth his physical strength, I felt perfectly

161

justified in shooting him, and as I staggered back from the blow, I reached for my pistol, intending to shoot him; he caught my hand, and by his superior strength and the disadvantage of my position, prevented me from getting it, and in the struggle the pistol fell and rolled down the stairs; while struggling for possession of the pistol, he called out "Judge, don't shoot me, I am unarmed"; but the moment he saw that the pistol was beyond my reach, he struck me again, this time with his naked fist, inflicting no damage, which satisfied me that the first blow was aided by some foreign substance in his hand. I threw my crippled arm about his neck, got his thumb in my mouth and proceeded to lacerate it to the best of my ability. In our struggle on the stairway, he got me down, his thumb still in my mouth, and in this position we were separated. Yet he told the *Telephone* reporter, in substance, that he knocked me down the stairs and that he supposed my friends picked me up and carried me away, which he knew, and others knew at the time he made it, that it was false. He has made other false statements about this matter that will be demonstrated on my trial. I waited until the excitement of mob violence had quieted down, as it was my duty to do, sent him a message by a friend, inviting him to meet me in a way in which all physical inequalities would be equalized, offering if he would do so, to apologize for the epithet I had applied to him; yet, unsatisfied with having forced the difficulty upon me, unsatisfied with having made a false report to the reporter of the *Telephone*, he refused to meet me, on the ground that he was NO FIGHTING MAN, and that there was NO ADEQUATE CAUSE FOR A DIFFICULTY.

These are the facts, and I hereby brand J. W. Harris, editor of the *Times-Herald*, as a liar, a coward, and a cur; as a man who has taken every advantage, who lies about difficulties that he has brought about himself, and then, like the craven cur that he is, refuses to meet the man he has wronged on equal terms; but as I understand, forts himself up in his office, where he could shoot me down from behind his cowardly breastworks without any danger to himself. I had no objection to his using his shotgun, if he had come into the alleyway back of his office, and allowed me to use mine on him. I thus brand him as unworthy of the respect of decent gentlemen and shall circulate this handbill throughout McLennan county so that in every community where he dares to carry his cowardly face and currish heart, they may know the proper estimate to put upon him. I am told by some of my friends that I will be assassinated by this cowardly cur, who will either shoot me from behind some breastworks or as I pass along the street. Assassination is what no man can protect himself from, if the assassin is determined. I pledge my friends, having done my duty to myself and this community, in exposing a liar, a coward, and a cur, that I will not hunt him, either in his office or anywhere else, but I have walked the streets of Waco for nearly thirty years without the fear of either brave men or assassins, and I will continue to do so. I have only this to say to my friends, if any cowardly advantage is taken of me and I am assassinated, I leave it to them to see that the cowardly assassin receives his just deserts; also, if anyone comes forward, after my assassination, and claims that he heard me make threats against J. W. Harris, treat him as an accessory before the fact, to my assassination, for I am not of the threatening kind, and have not made and will not make any threats against him.

G. B. Gerald

The outcome of the affair was related by Dr. W. O. Wilkes, whose diary, quoted below, recreates the dusty street, the bitter music of misunderstanding, and the hot sunlight of obligatory honor.

A week or two after the encounter between Gerald and Harris at the news office, W. A. Harris who was still my friend, asked me confidentially what I thought of the whole matter, and I was frank "and foolish" enough to tell him that, knowing Gerald as I did, either Gerald or J. W. would be killed before it was over. Gerald was old and in bad health, and soured by disappointment in his two sons and oldest daughter, and did not care for life; in fact, I heard it said that he wanted to die.

J. W. was sick, or pretended to be, for about three weeks, and remained at home, to avoid meeting Gerald. On the afternoon of November 19th I was standing in the front door of the drug store when J. W. passed, coming down from North 4th Street to cross Austin. He reached the curb and was about to step into the street when he suddenly stopped and turned back. Seeing me in the store door, to my surprise he came up and shook hands with me and stood by my side. I hadn't seen him in months and hadn't talked with him in a year, not since he had given up his life insurance connection and become editor to further his political ambitions; he now aspired to election to Congress, or so I was told.

He was nervous and very pale, which I thought was due to illness. Suddenly he said: "There is old Gerald across the street; what do you suppose he means to do?"

I looked across and saw Gerald sitting in his buggy, with his feeble-minded epileptic son, at the curb on the Fourth Street side of Sleeper Clifton's shoe store, diagonally across the street from us. I had not seen them before. I answered: "I don't know, J. W., but I am afraid you'll have trouble with him sooner or later."

Just then my sister-in-law came by and stopped to speak with me, and J. W. stepped back into the store beside the soda fountain. When my sister-in-law passed on I turned and walked back to where J. W. was standing, nervously tapping his foot on the floor. He turned quickly and went back to the store door to watch Gerald, and I followed him. In the meantime Gerald had driven up his buggy and turned the corner, and was now sitting, alone, in the buggy directly in front of Sleeper Clifton's store, his back towards us. In a minute the half-wit son quickly crossed the sidewalk to the buggy and leaned over and said something to his father, nodding his head towards us and looking directly at us. I knew that he had told his father that J. W. was at the drug store as well as if I had heard the words; and so did J. W.

Gerald turned and looked over his spectacles at us and immediately dropped the reins and jumped out of the buggy, into the middle of the street, and made a bee-line towards us.

I said "Look out, J. W., he's coming," and I walked hurriedly towards the back of the store, feeling sure that a fight was coming. As I passed W. B. Morrison and a clerk at the end of the first counter I said to them hurriedly, "Look out, there's going to be some shooting." Just then I heard a pistol shot and looking back saw J. W. with a pistol extended in his hand; then there were two other shots in quick succession, and as I passed behind the prescription counter I looked back and saw Gerald loom up at the edge of the sidewalk, and saw him deliberately fire and J. W. sank to the floor in front of the cigar stand. I was in direct line of Gerald's fire, but he shot only once and then turned back to cross the street to the other side where W. A. Harris was standing trying to shoot again. He had shot once as Gerald shot J. W. and was now holding his pistol in both hands trying to make it fire again but in his nervousness he probably did not let the trigger swing forward far enough. I had not seen him before and didn't know he was in the neighborhood. I went forward to the front of the store where J. W. was lying just in time to see Gerald fire the shot that killed W. A. instantly.

I called to the clerks to close the doors, and knelt down beside J. W. and asked him if he was hurt much. He answered, "I am mortally wounded, doctor." I said, "Oh, no. It can't be so bad as that." And he said, "Yes, I am mortally wounded; don't you hear the death rattle in my throat?"

What he thought was the death rattle was the air going in and out through a hole in his windpipe and lower part of his neck. The bullet had perforated it and lodged in the spinal cord, completely paralyzing him from the neck down. He was conscious and rational for several hours, but died before the next morning.

J. W.'s first shot lodged in Gerald's disabled arm, which he carried across his body when walking. J. W.

had a double-action self-cocking revolver which he was not familiar with, and he couldn't make it fire a second time. Then he pulled another pistol with his left hand and fired once, with his left hand, missing, and then he couldn't make it fire again. Gerald walked into the face of these two shots and received one from the rear from W. A. before he fired the first time. The ball from W. A.'s pistol, I was told, struck a metal button on Gerald's back and glanced off.

"Go Cork Yourselves"

CHAPTER 14

In his cold fury Gerald had approached so close to Bill Harris before firing that the dead man's collar had been set smouldering by the flame from the pistol.

It was a sobering thought that a man could walk out of his house on a sunny afternoon, alert and sensible, perhaps kiss his wife good-by—but more likely just call out casually the hour he expected to return— and within the hour become a grotesque burning doll in a rubbish-strewn gutter. There had been no music, no preparation, no time to say good-by or to ask that a cock be paid to Asclepius.

For most Wacoans, the double shooting served as a bitter climax to the Baylor-Brann feud, and they were anxious to lay the whole business to rest.

At the same time there were many people untiringly dedicated to erasing Brann and his *Iconoclast*

168

from Waco. He was a mounting irritant to their souls, a frustrating menace to their warm religious security, an anarchist armed with suasion and viciousness. Furthermore, he was a threat to complacency.

In many ways Brann's personality was one to add fuel to these fires. Especially after several drinks he could be offensively argumentative, immensely arrogant, and razor-tongued. With the immoderate fervor peculiar to reformists, he saw no view but his own, and his discussions were not debates but sarcasms laced with wit and devastating analogies.

Those who were "Brann's men" enjoyed the sport, but it was not an approach calculated to soothe the tempers of his enemies. They must have relished, for example, this tribute to Dr. Burleson.

Dr. Rufus C. Burleson is not a perfect man. He has not always treated the *Iconoclast* either with Christian charity or courtesy; but as men go, he's far above the average. While he was president of Baylor University its students did not get drunk. They were not encouraged to arm themselves and commit lawless acts of violence. All the good that is in Baylor University is due to his untiring efforts and self-sacrifice. There would be no Baylor University to-day but for Dr. Burleson; yet after nearly half a century of service, he has been pitched out and humiliated and lied about by creatures who are not worthy to breathe the same atmosphere. The Baptist fight is none of mine; but I am the champion of fair play; and I say here that even in his so-called "dotage," Dr. Burleson has more brains, more

169

good morals, more manhood, than have Carroll, Cranfill, and all their scurvy crew. If the enemies of Burleson triumph at the coming state convention, then the Baptist sect ought to perish from the earth. Shake, Doctor; Baylor has treated you a damned sight worse than it has treated me.

Although in the November issue of the *Iconoclast* the Apostle had indicated he would "drop the subject until another attempt is made to run me out of town," he swung back at Baylor in December. In one article, entitled "Speaking for Myself," he mentioned the hundreds of letters he had received suggesting that he move the *Iconoclast* to some more hospitable city. He declined these offers with thanks. "To the kindly offers of other cities to afford the *Iconoclast* an asylum and protect its editor from outrage, I will simply say that I do not consider either my property or my person in the slightest danger. A majority of the Texas people are both broad gauged and law-abiding. . . . I like the climate, and most of the people, and am in no hurry to move." He added that should he leave now it would be bruited about that he was driven out, "just as my brethren in Christ say I was driven out of San Antonio." Finally, he recommended to his readers the new contributors he was gathering to write for the paper. "Should the editor chance to swallow too much water the next time he is baptized, they can be depended upon to keep that flag of the *Iconoclast* afloat until the red-headed heir-apparent learns to write with one hand and shoot with the other. Let it go at that." He signed it in capitals: BRANN.

A more direct attack, published among the miscellaneous reflections he grouped under "Salmagundi," read as follows:

I noticed in one of the local papers that "Dallas wants Baylor," $50,000 to $75,000 worth. Doubtless I'm a hopeless heretic, but I don't believe a d--n word of it. If anybody thinks that Dallas will put up $25,000 cash to secure the removal thither of Baylor, he can find a man about these premises who will make him a 2 to 1 game that his believer is 'way off his base. Dallas doesn't want Baylor even a little bit. There isn't a town in this world that wants it except Waco. It is simply another Frankenstein monster that has destroyed its architect. Baylor spends no money here worth mentioning. Its students are chiefly forks-of-the-creek yaps who curry horses or run errands for their board and wear the same undershirt the year round. They take but two baths during their lifetime—one when they are born, the other when they are baptized. The institution is worth less than nothing to any town. It is what Ingersoll would call a storm-center of misinformation. It is the Alma Mater of mob violence. It is a chronic breeder of bigotry and bile. As a small Waco property owner, I will give it $1,000 any time to move to Dallas, and double that amount if it will go to Honolulu or hell. There is no bitterness in this, no desire to offend; it is simply a business proposition by a business man who realizes that Baylor is a disgrace to the community, is playing Old Man of the Sea to Waco's Sinbad. The town could well afford to give it $100,000 to "pull its freight."

Beginning with the January and February issues of 1898 Brann began to publish more and more contributions from his "bouquet of pansy blossoms." They were provocative and written with a flair for the current: Was the life of an actress a violation of the instincts of motherhood? Were city girls more liable to "fall into error" than country girls? Was Macaulay greater than Carlyle?

In February he again attacked Baylor and the Baptists in an essay headed "The Why and Wherefore." The city had offered a bonus of $15,000 to serve as the location of the Masonic Widows' and Orphans' Home, and the gift was declined. His enemies circulated the story that the home was not established in Waco because the *Iconoclast* was published there. The story was published in the local papers, and Brann decided to reply.

Waco recently offered a bonus—or made a bluff of offering it—of $15,000 for the location of the Masonic Widows' and Orphans' Home. Waco is forever making a large piebald ass of herself. . . . Were the majestic universe for sale at $10 cash she'd fail to make connections—would get hopelessly sidetracked while conferring, banqueting, whereasing, resoluting, perorating, and otherwise agitating the atmosphere while getting ready to let someone else begin. . . . Waco is emphatically a pinhook fisherman. Although its natural

172

advantages are superior to those of any other Texas city it is sixth in size. That's because it imagines that it can work industrial wonders by drinking toasts and feeding its face. . . .

The Home did not come to Waco because the Masons declined to commit their loved ones to the care of a community that has ostentatiously eulogized a brace of would-be assassins who "double-banked" a crippled Confederate colonel—who shot him in the back then became so badly frightened that they couldn't work their guns and were killed while trying to escape the righteous punishment of their cowardly crime. . . .

The Home did not come to Waco because a lot of splenetic-hearted hypocrites and pietistical dead-beats —who should have been hanged with their own umbilicular cords at birth—have given the place a bad name which it will take a dozen years to live down. The cry raised by certain mischief-making little fuzzy-wuzzies that Waco lost the Home because of the *Iconoclast* was simply a stupid prevarication made with malice prepense. It is barely possible that a few professional log-rollers for other locations did mouth somewhat about this magazine—shoot their smooth-bore bazoos at "Brannville"—but their goose-gabble sawed absolutely no ice. The *Iconoclast* has cost Waco nary a nick. Together with its auxiliary publications it draws hither more money from beyond Waco's legitimate trade territory than do all other institutions combined. It asked no bonus to come and it will not go until it gets a real good ready. There are not Baptists enough in Texas to drive it out of this town. If they kill the editor, another and a better man will step into his shoes and continue the old fight against hypocrites

173

and humbugs, against all that loveth and maketh a lie. . . .

Just a little more of this malicious persecution, this sanctified misrepresentation, and Baylor will receive an iconoclastic revelation that will make the one engineered by the lamented John of Patmos seem like an iridescent dream. If there be yet a God in Israel or sense of decency or justice remaining in the human heart, I can come precious near making that pseudo-sacrosanct institution tuck its fleabitten tail between its hinder legs and flee unto the mountains of Hepsidam, where the lion roareth and the whang-doodle mourneth for its first-born. Sweet Christians, if you want peace, I prithee go cork yourselves.

"Come Along, Mr. Brann!"

CHAPTER 15

 Perhaps because the times seemed appropriate for a vacation, or perhaps because recent incidents had made Brann a figure of national interest, Ward persuaded the Apostle to undertake an extended lecture tour. The first talk was to be given Saturday night, April 2, 1898, in the San Antonio Opera House. From there the tour would include Houston, Galveston, and New Orleans and perhaps swing northward to Chicago.

It is probable that Brann was reluctant to leave Waco at a time when his enemies could accuse him of cowardice, for the threats upon him were as thick as the bluebonnets in the meadows. More important to him, however, was his wife, Carrie—"Midget"—whose nerves had been completely frayed by the procession of tragedies.

In addition to random shootings and beatings, Baylor boys would occasionally gather in a menacing mob before the stately house and shout taunts and abuse until dispersed by the police. A former neighbor of Brann's remembers one occasion when the boys were so unruly that firehoses had to be turned on them before they retreated.

For a woman to whom social position and the social graces were important, Carrie's existence in Waco must have been a nightmare to her. She became more and more of a recluse—a slight, harried woman whose only consolations were motherhood and her flower garden.

To free his wife from every care during their trip, Brann decided to leave Gracie and Billy at home. Now they could afford to stay at the finest hotels, dine in the best restaurants. The tour would be like a second honeymoon—a kind of Jim dash separating the first harried and disconnected paragraphs of their lives from the more leisured, satisfying prose that would record their future years in the lovely brick home set among the gardens and the great oak and cedar trees.

Actually his own nerves needed a rest, too. There was bravado and a sort of security in the pistol he learned to carry, but when he practiced whirling, drawing, and firing under Judge Gerald's tutelage, he would finish exhausted and shaking. The enemy was not "men"—the enemy was cant and sham, and who could slay them with lead?

Yes, the tour would be a tonic for them all, and

Brann was in excellent spirits the day before they were to leave. He spent the morning and most of the afternoon at home with his family and Bill Ward. Jim Shaw's daughter had agreed to stay at "The Oaks" and care for the children, and Carrie spent the last afternoon showing her the lawn sprinklers, the supplies of linens, and the innumerable details that were important to Billy and Gracie's life. She prepared an itinerary so that she could be reached by telegraph in case of emergency, and she made menus for Billy's diet. For her, it was a wonderful dream come true.

At four o'clock in the afternoon Brann was driven to town in his hack by his Negro factotum, Lee, and he told Ward he would be back well before six. Ward needed the carriage to meet his brother and some friends who were due to arrive in town by train later that evening.

But almost two hours later, when Brann had not yet returned, Ward took the streetcar down Fifth and into town. He ran into John Guerin, walked with him toward the depot, and met Brann at the corner of Fourth Street and Banker's Alley. They were joined for a few moments by Joe Earp, a "young fellow from the western part of the county" who was curious to know the editor of the *Iconoclast*. Earp, Brann, and Ward chatted together as they walked to Laneri's Saloon, and then, as Earp reported, "they went inside and I left them."

A short time later, Ward led the way out again to Fourth Street. He and Brann crossed it and walked northward. They passed a barber shop, and they passed Finnie Williams' real estate office. Ahead of them the sun's rays were still bright on Waco.

Neither of them saw a large man named Tom Davis lunge to the door of Williams' office, a pistol in his hand. A shot rang out—pain stabbed Brann's back. He whirled and drew his gun. He saw a man ten feet away, crouched, preparing to fire again. Brann squeezed the trigger, and the blast jerked the long barrel upward. Davis staggered, and Brann saw Ward leap at him and catch the wavering muzzle of the pistol with his hand. Davis fired and the bullet ripped through Ward's hand and into the air.

Davis fell to one knee. Brann fired again and again, as fast as he could pull the trigger. Davis returned the shots, and the sound echoed in Brann's ears. Acrid smoke stung his eyes, but he kept pulling the trigger of his empty pistol, although he could no longer see his attacker. Then he felt suddenly weak and ill, and he dropped the gun to the pavement.

A uniformed figure appeared beside him and roughly grasped his arm. Brann recognized Sam Hall, a policeman. "You're under arrest!" he heard Hall shout at him excitedly. "Come along, Mr. Brann!"

Very faint, he let Hall guide him toward Austin Street. Soon another hand grasped his left arm.

"Ward," he said. "What happened to Ward?"

"He's all right," a voice replied. "They're fixing his hand."

Brann's eyes kept blurring so that he had to shake his head to clear his sight. Then, little by little, the numbness in his back went away and a great surging ache swelled inside him. It squeezed against his lungs and took away his breath. It clamped against his heart, and he could feel it strain at each beat. Dazedly he turned his head toward Hall. "I've been wounded," he whispered, and all the while his feet were rising and falling automatically on the pavement.

Now there were stone steps and then a big room. Excited voices echoing roughly. "By God, he *is* wounded!" "Lay him down here!" "No, put him here."

He felt many hands, more gentle now, and in a moment he was lying face down. They fumbled at his clothes in back, and he could hear cloth tearing. "Right where his suspenders crossed!" "By God, it don't look bad, but look at his shoes—full of blood!" "Hello, doc. Hello, doc. Hello, doc."

Then a carriage and the great rump of a horse and the sound of horse's hooves. Then floating by a stair rail and into a bed—his own bed.

When he woke and opened his eyes there were great flames of light flashing from the little lamps in the room. He wrenched his body back and forth.

He felt a hand on his forehead and relaxed like a child. "Who is it?" a *News* reporter heard him ask.

"It's me, love." It was Midget.

His voice was barely a whisper. "It is nothing," he said. "This will all pass away. I will be better and we will walk together on the lawn just as we used to do." . . .

Epilogue

 William Cowper Brann, shot through the left groin, in the right foot, and through the middle of the back, was marched by Officers Hall and Durie two and a half blocks to the city hall. At the conclusion of this trip, which medical authorities have said probably contributed greatly to his death, it was observed that Brann was badly wounded, and he was "laid upon a couch" until 7:20 P.M., when friends took him home to "The Oaks."

A contemporary recalls that the parlor furniture was shrouded with dust covers in anticipation of the trip and that Brann was laid on a sofa in this room surrounded by looming, shapeless, and white forms. He was attended by Drs. Foscue, Hale, Graves, and C. E. Smith.

As the evening wore on, he seemed to recover from shock and improve generally, but at 11:00 P.M. he be-

cording to the ritual of the Knights of the Maccabees, and one of the more outstanding floral tributes was a large wreath of red and white flowers sent by Artesian Tent No. 6, of which Davis was a member.

His pallbearers were Judge W. H. Jenkins, J. E. Boynton, F. B. Williams, J. N. Harris, A. C. Riddle, J. K. Rose, J. H. Gouldy, W. H. Deaton, Robert Wright, S. F. Kirksey, Major A. Symes, and James I. Moore.

Shortly after his death, Brann's friends subscribed for a large monument in the form of a granite obelisk bearing a lamp of truth. One side of the obelisk bears a bas-relief profile of Brann carved in marble. Tom Davis' grave in the family enclosure is unmarked, but an aged Negro who helped dig the grave pointed out the exact site to the author.

It is fascinating and frustrating to attempt a reconstruction of the movements of Brann and Davis during the hour before their duel. Several accounts indicate that the two did meet earlier in the afternoon and that Brann cursed Davis, who was a vocal anti-Brann citizen. Other accounts say that Brann merely paused and glared at Davis. And still others fail to mention a meeting of any kind. Yet if Brann knew Davis, how could his constant companion, Ward, have this to say after the shooting: "I do not wish to speak ill of the dead, therefore I shall have but little to say of Mr. Davis. My acquaintance with him was brief; I never met him but once—when he was shooting another man, *in the back.*"

This fact, certainly, is borne out by an overwhelming number of witnesses, plus Brann's wound in the back.

Why did Davis do it? There is no pat answer. He had a daughter attending Baylor, and one school of thought contends that his action was one of private vengeance for a slandered child. But if so, it was very delayed vengeance. Another theory is that Davis hated Brann for reviving a rumor that in his more carefree cowpunching days Davis was in the vicinity during a stage holdup at Lampasas. Still another theory is that Davis, who had local political ambitions, would surely corral the Baptist vote (which meant a shoo-in) if he performed a service for them such as exterminating their archenemy.

Perhaps we overcomplicate the issue. Maybe Davis simply couldn't stand the sight of his enemy walking arrogantly up the street—and so grabbed a gun and shot him. It was not so uncommon in Texas in the 1890's.

Ward left Waco soon after the tragedy. His wounded hand was treated at a drugstore, and he was jailed the night of the affair in lieu of $4,000 bond. He was released in time to attend the funeral Sunday, and the May *Iconoclast*—the last—was issued under his editorial supervision "as a labor of love."

Gradually, as the years passed, the passionate hatreds cooled and the wounds began to heal. Preyed upon by seers and clairvoyants, a nerve-wracked, helpless Carrie was taken to Oklahoma by her in-laws to begin a fresh life. Her flight toward the stars with the stormy, moody, dependent genius she so adored was to become a brittle, cherished memory—more evanescent than the words he wrote for the world, but far far more precious to her than a thousand books or ten thousand cadenced phrases.

Source Material

 The incidents in this biography are based, without fictional embellishment or conjecture, upon the following sources and upon interviews or correspondence with the gracious people listed here.

Brann's Iconoclast (complete files). Waco, Brann Publishing Co., 1894–98.
Brann's Scrapbook. Waco, Baylor University, Texas Collection.
Brann's Speeches and Lectures. Waco, Knight Printing Co.
Potiphar's Wife. San Antonio, Guessaz and Ferlat, 1894.
The Works of Brann the Iconoclast. 12 vols. New York, The Brann Publishers, Inc., 1919.

Anonymous. *The Brann Episode.* Waco, Baylor University, Texas Collection.

Armstrong, James, Jr. *Brann X-Rayed*. San Antonio, Eureka Printing Co.

————. *Broadsides for Brann*. San Antonio, Eureka Printing Co., 1897.

Burleson, Rufus. *The Brazilian Girl and Baylor University*. Waco, 1895. Baylor University, Texas Collection.

Cocke, J. W. *Six-Shooter Junction* (unpublished manuscript). Waco, Baylor University, Texas Collection.

Conger, Roger N. *Highlights of Waco History*. Waco, Hill Printing and Stationery Co., 1945.

Cranfill, J. B. *Shaw: Free Thinker and Biographer of Brann*. Waco, Baylor University, Texas Collection.

Cutter's Guide to the City of Waco. Waco, 1894. Baylor University, Texas Collection.

Dawson, Joseph. *Brann the Iconoclast, 30 Years After*. Waco, Baylor University, Texas Collection.

Fletcher, Edward Garland. *Brann the Playwright*. Austin, University of Texas, 1941.

Gage, Harold. *This Man Brann*. Waco, Baylor University, Texas Collection.

Nicholson, Dan. *The Brann-Davis Duel*. Waco, Baylor University, Texas Collection.

Randolph, John. "The Apostle of the Devil" (unpublished Master's thesis, Vanderbilt University). Nashville, Tenn., Joint University Libraries, 1941.

Whitaker, John R. "W. C. Brann, His Life and Influence" (unpublished Master's thesis, University of Texas). Waco, Baylor University, Texas Collection.

Early newspaper files and scrapbooks, Waco Public Library.

The author expresses gratitude for correspondence with Mrs. Charles Knight, whose brother married Gracie Brann; Mrs. Iris Petroff, Gracie's daughter; Mrs. Janet Kopperl, a friend of Carrie's; Mrs. Pauline Brann, who married Billy; Donald L. Brann, Brann's grandson; Mrs. Maud Gerald Richardson, Judge Gerald's daughter; Ed Kilman, of the *Houston Post*; Tom L. McCullough, city attorney of Waco and eyewitness of both the Gerald-Harris and the Brann-Davis shootings; Harry Burkhalter, of the *San Antonio Light*; and many others who have helped by furnishing material.

A random and certainly incomplete list of persons interviewed (who are herewith tendered my renewed thanks) includes Harry Provence; Roger Conger; Judge Allan Sanford; Judge J. W. Cocke; Tom Hamilton; Roy Durie, son of police officer Durie; J. R. Collier; Pat Neff; Dr. Guy B. Harrison; Chapin M. Seley; Henry Lovelace; W. G. Barrett; Mrs. Walter Reese, Sr.; Ed Carter, J. M. Pittillo; J. D. Williamson; Mrs. A. L. Endt; Mrs. A. D. Brinkerhoff; Robert P. Dupree; Frank and Helen Baldwin; Mrs. H. W. Houk; Mrs. W. O. Wilkes; Mrs. Lillian Russell; J. Frank Dobie; Edmunds Travis; Roy Bedichek; J. R. Torrance; and Dr. John Arthur Ray, a contemporary Baylor student who attended the Slattery lecture, witnessed the kidnaping incident on the Baylor campus, and boarded with young George Scarborough.

Index

192